SMALL BUSINESS FINANCIAL MANAGEMENT

ABOUT THE AUTHOR

Ivan Houston is a Chartered Accountant, Chartered Tax Advisor, and co-owner of Scholes Chartered Accountants, an accountancy business that helps people who want to create and grow great small businesses.

Ivan is a passionate advocate for the UK small business community. He is a graduate of the Goldman Sachs *10,000 Small Businesses* UK programme, a prize winner in the examinations of the Association of Taxation Technicians, and a mentor for the Institute of Chartered Accountants of Scotland Foundation which supports talented accountancy students from disadvantaged backgrounds.

Ivan lives in Orkney with his wife Amy, daughters Beatrice, Jenny and Florence, and assorted animals.

Contact Ivan by e:mail at ivan@scholesca.co.uk.

SMALL BUSINESS FINANCIAL MANAGEMENT

How to organise and manage the finances in your small business

Ivan Houston

Copyright © 2019 Ivan Houston

All rights reserved

ISBN-13: 9781693294778

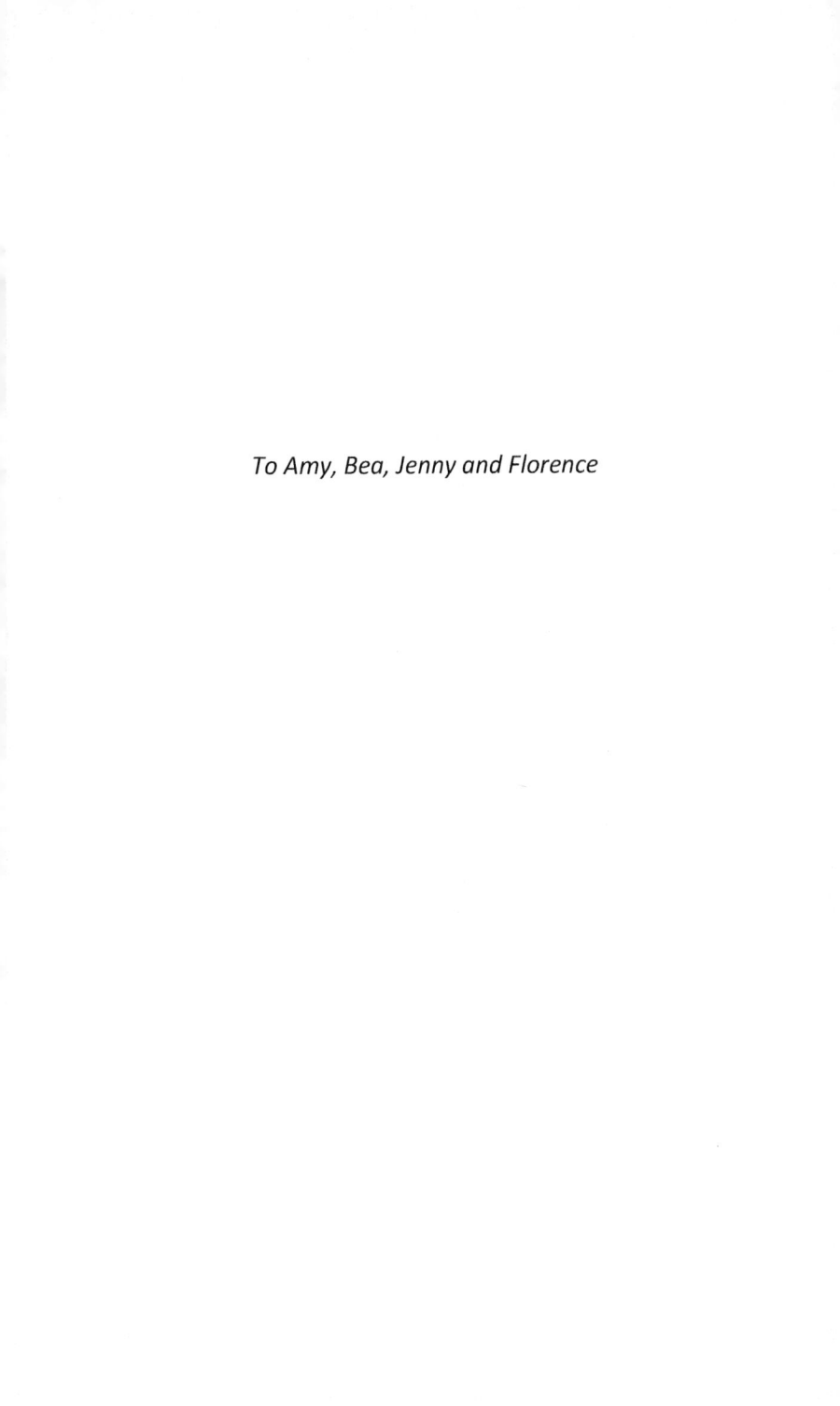

To Amy, Bea, Jenny and Florence

Contents

Foreword xi

Preface xv

Introduction 1

Part 1: Basic financial processes

1 Why basic financial processes matter 9
2 What is a business? 11
3 The sales process 13
4 The purchases process 22
5 The expense claim process 31
6 The payroll process 35
7 The construction industry scheme 43

8 Banking processes **46**
9 Tax compliance processes **53**
10 Fixed asset management processes **58**
11 Stock management processes **64**
12 Nominal ledger processes **70**
13 The accounts production process **79**
14 Budgeting & forecasting processes **81**
15 Administration **83**
16 Choosing accounting software **85**
17 Internal controls for the small business **90**

Part 2: Understanding accounts
18 Why understanding your accounts is vital 97
19 Introducing: the primary financial statements **99**
20 The value of accounts **101**
21 Management accounts vs statutory accounts **103**
22 Whose job is it to prepare the accounts? **105**
23 Basic accounting concepts **107**
24 The balance sheet **111**
25 The profit & loss account **126**
26 Reporting income and expenditure - important concepts **136**

27 The cash flow statement **139**

28 Preparing and interpreting the cash flow statement **143**

29 Notes to the accounts **145**

30 Qualitative aspects of financial statements.......................... **147**

Part 3: Managing the finances

31 Knowledge is power **153**

32 Managing cash flows... **155**

33 Budgeting & forecasting **160**

34 Profit margins **169**

35 Breakeven sales quantity... **175**

36 Monitoring performance against budget/ forecast............... **177**

37 Common problems with management accounts **184**

38 Key performance indicators.. **189**

39 How ratio analysis can help you manage the finances **194**

40 Financial performance ratios **197**

41 Financial position ratios.. **204**

42 Managing your working capital **207**

43 Cash flow crisis management.. **210**

44 The value of pre year-end planning **214**

45 Strengthening the balance sheet... **220**

46 Dividends – getting the details right **224**

Part 4: Making big financial decisions

47 First, select your team **229**
48 Choosing a business structure.. **231**
49 Paying yourself **236**
50 Pricing and customers **241**
51 Registering for VAT **245**
52 Employing staff **249**
53 Marketing... **255**
54 Buying business premises **259**
55 Raising finance... **266**
56 The impact of taxation **275**
57 Selling up... **285**
58 Choosing an accountant **288**

Glossary.. **292**
Index **306**

Foreword

In Ivan's preface to this book, he describes its inspiration being a workshop he attended during which 'the lecturer painstakingly explained the very basics of business financial management'. That lecturer was me.

Since 2011, through my involvement in programmes such as the Goldman Sachs 10,000 Small Businesses UK programme and others that we have delivered at Aston Business School, I have worked with more than 1,000 small business leaders and from this experience I can testify that this book is long overdue and will be a useful companion to all small business leaders.

Few would argue that good financial management is vital for the survival let alone success of any small business. Yet financial management skills and an understanding of accounting information and concepts are widely neglected by small business leaders, including many who in other ways would rightly be regarded as highly successful entrepreneurs.

One reason for this may be that the subject of accounting and finance is often perceived to be dry and impenetrable. As a result, even in small businesses in which internal accounting information is produced we typically find it is not used to its greatest potential in the management of the business. And in some small businesses, internal accounting information is not even produced at all. Indeed, in some cases, the only accounting information which is produced is for year-end statutory and tax compliance purposes, and many small business leaders are only too happy to delegate this task to their external accountants, with their prime concern being merely that their accountants will seek to ensure (through legitimate means of course!) that their personal tax liability is minimised.

But financial management is much more than this and just imagine how much more successful business leaders could be if only they had a greater command of their business' finances!

This book will help the business leader improve their financial management skills, and thereby improve the likelihood of business success. It will also help the business leader's confidence with the financial side of their business, and in some cases may even enable them to sleep more easily at night!

The book will be helpful for beginners and for those with more experience. It is practical and includes the key features of the current legal and tax regime affecting UK small businesses. It is also comprehensive in its coverage, dealing with the key accounting and finance topics relevant to any small business leader: understanding financial processes; interpreting financial information; choosing and using key financial metrics; and using key financial tools such as

Foreword

break-even analysis and cash flow forecasts to help with important business decisions.

It also addresses the common mistakes and misconceptions which I encounter in my workshops which include:

- mixing the terms 'creditors' and 'debtors' (we owe creditors; debtors owe us)

- believing that if a business is profitable it must also be generating positive cash flows (which is not necessarily true)

- confusing the 'profit and loss account reserve' (or 'retained profit') with a pot of cash available to be spent (which it is not!)

I congratulate Ivan on this excellent contribution to the sources of guidance and support on the subject of financial management for small business leaders.

Matt Davies, October 2019.

Senior Teaching Fellow, Aston Business School.

Finance Faculty Lead for Goldman Sachs *10,000 Small Businesses* UK.

Project Lead for the 'Financial Education for Future Entrepreneurs' project, funded by the Erasmus+ Programme of the European Union, the main output of which is 'Count FEFE' a free to download game for supporting the development of accounting and finance skills for business.

Preface

In the summer of 2017 I sat in a classroom with thirty five fellow small business owners, as the lecturer (also a Chartered Accountant) painstakingly explained the very basics of business financial management.

As far as I could tell, apart from the lecturer and I nobody in the room had any formal financial training – and all seemed to have very little grasp of even quite basic financial matters. All this, despite the fact that my classmates were, without exception, amazingly talented, highly successful individuals running some of the best small businesses in the UK.

In that moment, I resolved to write a book about small business financial management, for the benefit of small business owners everywhere – but particularly those with no formal financial training. And here it is.

Ivan Houston, October 2019

Introduction

Financial management matters

This book is all about the financial basics you need to know and apply to run your small business more effectively.

In the following chapters I'll describe the basic financial procedures most small businesses need; show you how to understand and interpret accounts; discuss simple techniques to manage your business finances; and explore some of the big financial decisions business owners might make.

In the UK there are around 5.5 million small businesses, each one making a great contribution to the lives of ordinary people just like you and me, providing meaningful employment, sustaining families and communities, and meeting the needs and wants of consumers and other businesses small and large. Our country would be immeasurably poorer without the amazing contributions and ceaseless efforts of the small business sector.

Yet the surprising truth is that many small business owners would do an even better job of serving their customers, employees, and communities, if only they could manage the financial side of their businesses more effectively. It's partly for the want of time, but also, I believe, for the want of knowledge and skills. That's not a criticism, by the way; most small business owners never receive any formal training in financial matters.

I am a director at an accountancy firm, Scholes CA, which specialises in assisting people who want to create, manage and grow great small businesses. From my own experience I know that accountants can and do make a massive contribution to the small business sector, advising, informing, guiding, explaining, even coercing and cajoling bewildered clients to take better care of the money side of things. But accountants are busy people, and they can't be by your side 24/7 (that would be expensive, for a start!).

What's more, when it comes to financial literacy, sometimes the gulf between the business owner and their accountant is just so wide that, almost inevitably, there are a lot of financial issues that just never get discussed or addressed. In extreme cases, the business owner (and, by extension, their accountant) may even be unaware of the true scale of any financial problems or improvement opportunities within the business.

Occasionally, I suspect, the poor business owner is just too embarrassed to admit that they don't *really* know what a bank reconciliation is, or how hire purchase actually works, or what a balance sheet really tells you. They may even feel that their accountant is just too busy to answer such basic questions – which is a real shame because an accountant really is able help with that kind of stuff too!

This book is my attempt to help small business owners fill in the missing pieces of the financial puzzle – both to fill in the gaps in their financial knowledge and practice; and to narrow the knowledge gulf between themselves and their accountant, so that both parties can enjoy a more fruitful professional relationship. And ultimately, to help hard working business owners create, manage and grow great small businesses.

I hope you find this book helpful and informative. Like all progressive business owners, I recognise there is always room for improvement so I would really welcome your feedback on how I can make the next edition even better. You can contact me at ivan@scholesca.co.uk.

What this book is about

To manage your business finances effectively, you need three things:

- Basic financial processes and procedures to safeguard your business's assets, comply with the law, and produce the financial information you need to be able to manage and grow your business;

- Procedures to summarise, monitor and interpret the financial information at your fingertips; and

- The ability to asses if everything is "on track" financially, so that if it is not you are in a position to do something about it.

So, this book is all about:

1. Basic financial processes – what are the processes and procedures you need to follow to deal with sales, purchases, customers and suppliers, banking and so on, including procedures for creating useful financial information; who should do what and when?

2. Understanding your accounts – what are the main financial reports, and how are they used? We will look at some financial words that accountants use and try to demystify them; we examine some important financial concepts; and we will also look at how to interpret what the financial reports mean – what can they tell us about your business's financial performance and position?

3. Managing the finances – we'll look at managing cash inflows and outflows; setting budgets; establishing important financial measures that you'll want to track; pricing; and a variety of other management subjects.

4. Decision making – finally we'll examine some of the key financial decisions that a small business owner might need to make, including taking on staff, registering for VAT, and buying premises.

Depending on your specific area(s) of interest, please feel welcome to dip in and out of the different chapters as you wish. For the most part the chapters are pretty "self-contained". Having said that, the later chapters do assume a certain amount of financial knowledge, so if you're a *total* beginner – start at the beginning!

PART 1

BASIC FINANCIAL PROCESSES

1

Why basic financial processes matter

When it comes to organising your business's finances, most of the advice and most of the books advocate a sort of "top down" approach where the business owner is meant to start with a nice, detailed business plan, then set out some detailed financial projections, then get all the processes and procedures set up.

Often what happens in reality is that you entrepreneurial types start off by selling some stuff, then gradually putting some sort of procedures in place bit by bit, encouraged by your poor, long suffering accountant.

It really evolves over time, and a business plan, if it ever features, often only arrives months or years later (sometimes at the behest of whichever bank or grant funding body has been asked to stump up some money!).

Whichever way you approach it though, the truth is you need to get your financial procedures in shape, as soon as possible.

Getting a solid financial foundation in place is a prerequisite for just about everything else – understanding how, and where, your business is making (or losing) money; complying with tax and accounting rules; and knowing what you need to do to achieve whatever outcomes you're working towards.

Even if making a profit is not your primary aim – even if your goal is simply to stay afloat, or run a social enterprise, whatever it is – the truth is that your business won't be sustainable if you don't stay on top of the finances.

2

What is a business?

To understand and make sense of the finances, it's helpful, first of all, to consider one question: what is a business? Essentially, a business is a series of processes – something goes in, something gets done, something comes out the other end. In other words, inputs, activities, and outputs. Those processes are operated by people and/or machines. The processes are (or should be) set up to achieve certain specific outcomes. That's all a business is, really!

Let me give you some examples:

- Buying goods – a purchases process - might involve deciding what to order (the input); phoning a supplier to make the order (the activity); and receiving the goods (the output).

- Selling goods – a sales process – might involve taking an order (the input); preparing the order for despatch (the activity); and despatching the goods to the customer (the output).

Thinking about a business in this way is a useful way of making sense of any organisation, large or small. Whilst this might seem kind of obvious, in order to establish robust financial procedures and lay the foundations for effective financial management and control, you firstly need to understand all the different processes that happen in your business. If you don't know what's happening in your business, you definitely won't be able to manage it effectively!

In the following chapters we'll look at the main *financial* processes that go on in most businesses. Of course, some of the activities that happen in a business are not necessarily financial – or not overtly so. But for the most part the things your business does - the buying, transforming, managing, selling, communicating, distributing, researching, employing, wheeling and dealing – all have financial implications of one sort or another.

Let's have a look at those financial processes in some detail.

3

The sales process

Explaining the sales process

Your business will (presumably) sell goods or services to customers. It will therefore have a sales process, which might include some or all of the following steps:

- Identifying a potential customer;
- Agreeing terms of business with the customer;
- Taking an order from the customer;
- Fulfilling the order;
- Updating stock records (where applicable);
- Invoicing the customer;

- Getting paid by the customer;
- Banking the money received;
- Making and keeping a record of the transactions; and
- Reporting the transactions (e.g. to the business owners, investors, lenders, HMRC).

Consider for a moment which of these things your business does (or which of these things you intend to do, if you are setting up a new business). They are all steps in the sales process – inputs, activities, or outputs.

The eagle-eyed among you will observe that many of the steps outlined above can be broken down into more steps, or be connected to other processes going on in a business. Take, for example, the step "fulfilling the order" – what might this entail? If your business manufactures, this might involve checking if the goods are in stock or if you need to make them; maybe buying more materials, producing the finished goods, despatching the goods to the customer, updating the stock records, and so on. If you run a service business, this might involve assigning staff to perform the service, scheduling dates, monitoring the time they spend delivering the service, getting feedback from the customer, and so on.

This illustrates exactly why it is beneficial to think about your business as a series of processes. By considering the activities that you (and any staff) undertake, and the relationship between all those different activities, you can build a deeper understanding of how everything in your business fits together; what works and what doesn't; what's crucial and what's not.

We'll discuss all the main processes in this section of the book. The sales process is a great place to start.

The aims of the sales process

What's the point of the sales process? From a financial perspective, you probably want to:

- Be paid a good price for your products or services;
- Foster customer loyalty (so your customers keep spending);
- Get paid as soon as possible to assist cash flow;
- Get paid on a timely basis and avoid bad debts;
- Make sure the money received is kept safely and securely;
- Prevent financial losses due to fraud or error;
- Distribute your products or services as efficiently as possible;
- Comply with the law, including tax laws; and
- Record and report the transactions accurately, promptly and efficiently.

If your business already does all these things, well done. Nevertheless, please read on...

Cash vs credit sales

Your business might make sales and get paid immediately. We call these "cash sales" (although that's a bit of a misnomer because it also includes sales where your customers pay you with a debit or credit card or by cheque, as well as using cash). It may make sales and get paid at some later point (in other words sales "credit sales"). Or it may do both. However it makes sales, though, your business will need some robust, basic sales processes.

Cash sales

For sales where you get paid immediately, you need a way to record each transaction at the point of sale. There are several reasons why:

- So you have an accurate record of sales made for financial monitoring and reporting purposes;

- To comply with tax and reporting rules; and

- To be able to check that the money your business makes ends up in the bank account (or is otherwise accounted for) – in other words to help prevent/ detect the loss of the cash due to theft or other reasons.

Retailers normally use a till system to record cash takings. If the business takes any cash out of the till for any reason – typically to pay wages or suppliers' bills – a full record should be made, and copies of relevant supplier invoices should be retained.

On a regular (usually daily or at least weekly) basis, the cash/ cheques in the till should be counted, reconciled (i.e. checked) back to the expected total per the till roll totals, and banked. The expected total for this purpose should of course take account of any cash taken out of the till, as discussed above.

Unless you, as the business owner, are actually operating the till, you really should "segregate" the roles of operating the till and performing the daily cash count/ reconciliation, since this reduces the risk that an unscrupulous employee might pocket some of the takings and then cover their tracks. I'm not questioning the integrity of your staff, dear reader – but trust me when I say it does happen. Much, much too often.

Credit sales

For sales made to customers on credit, you need a paper trail. Each time a sale is made, a sales invoice will need to be prepared and despatched to the customer, either at the time of the sale or else soon afterwards. You should always keep a copy for your own records too.

Your sales invoice should include:

- Your business name, address, contact details;
- A unique reference number (start at 1 and go up from there);
- The date of issue;
- The name and details of the customer who bought the goods/ received the service;

- A description of the goods or services supplied;
- The amount due; and
- Details of any credit terms (e.g. payment within 30 days).

If your business is VAT registered, your sales invoices will need to carry additional information specified by law, including your VAT registration number, the amount of VAT charged, and so on. E:mail me at ivan@scholesca.co.uk for further details.

As well as issuing sales invoices, you will also need a way to track which invoices have been paid and which remain outstanding. If you don't do this, your business might not get paid on time – or at all. At its most simplistic, this could mean keeping a separate file of invoices that are paid and unpaid, and writing on the copy invoices when they have been paid so you don't lose track.

Depending on your business, you may also decide to issue statements of account to customers periodically. The statements summarise outstanding invoices, credits, and any unallocated cash receipts/ refunds.

You will need to routinely identify and chase customers when their invoices become overdue and this is one of the most important financial procedures of all if you make sales on credit, because if you don't get paid on time (or at all), your business may fail. That's a hard fact of business, so make getting paid an absolute top priority at all times.

Receipts from customers that come in as cash or cheques should be banked as promptly as possible, and the details recorded on the pay-in book stub.

Let's now consider some of the broader financial processes associated with making sales.

Taking on new customers and granting credit

Depending on your line of business, you may want to be selective about who you take on as a customer, and what work you do for them; also about how much credit you will offer (in terms of amounts and days credit) to new or existing customers. Customers who end up paying late – or not at all – can cause significant cash flow problems and financial loss to your business.

Do also consider more broadly the terms on which you do business. If your business sells services, can you structure the terms so that you get paid earlier, or paid in stages, or via some sort of subscription – rather than getting paid only when the job is done?

Consider also *how* you would like to get paid. Can you insist that all customers pay you by Direct Debit or Standing Order, in order to improve cash flow and reduce the likelihood of bad debts? Or are you happy to take payment in whatever form the customer prefers?

Despatching the goods/ delivering the service

Most businesses need a way to record when goods are despatched to customers (or services are delivered) to help ensure accurate sales invoices are issued on a timely basis, and to make sure the financial records, including stock and VAT records (where applicable), are accurately stated.

Consider whether you need to produce goods despatched notes (and returns notes for any items subsequently returned by customers). If you are running a service business, do you need to operate a timesheet system to determine how much to bill your customers? Or a job costing system if your business constructs/ manufactures items for customers?

Recording sales, returns, and sales receipts

Your business should maintain a record of its sales, any returns, and money received from/ refunded to customers. Most businesses nowadays use accounting software products like Quickbooks or Xero to help record all their financial transactions, indeed in the UK this is mandated for many VAT registered businesses.

If your business is not required to keep records digitally and you really do not wish to do so, then a handwritten record of sales and bank/ cash receipts (and indeed purchases and bank/ cash payments) is really the *absolute* minimum.

Unless you as the business owner are responsible for all aspects of the sales process, you should wherever possible segregate the roles of making sales, invoicing customers, banking the sales receipts and recording transactions on the accounting system, since this reduces the risk of fraud and error.

Other income

Your business might also sometimes receive money from sources other than sales – for example bank interest, or government grants, or tax refunds. These receipts should also be entered into your accounting system so that you have a complete record of all receipts, from whatever source.

Monitoring outstanding debtors

If you record all your credit sales on accounting software, it should be possible to monitor and identify any overdue amounts by producing – and reviewing – an "aged debtors" report on a regular basis. The aged debtor report lists all outstanding (i.e. unpaid) customer invoices, with a breakdown by age – invoices raised in the last 30 days, 30-60 days, 60-90 days and over 90 days.

If your business makes significant amounts of sales on credit, then you – or someone on your management team – should be doing this regularly, at least monthly.

4

The purchases process

We've looked at sales, now it's time to think about purchases – what procedures will you need to make, record and pay for the things your business needs to buy.

Explaining the purchases process

If your business buys anything at all, it will have a purchases process, which might include some or all of the following steps:

- Identifying the need to buy something;
- Establishing a budget to spend;
- Selecting a supplier and agreeing terms;
- Ordering the goods or services;

- Receiving the goods or services;
- Updating the stock records (where applicable);
- Being charged by the supplier;
- Paying the supplier;
- Making and keeping a record of the transactions; and
- Reporting the transactions.

The aims of the purchases process

The purchases process, like the sales process, has several different aims. You'll probably be looking to:

- Buy only what is needed;
- Buy on favourable price and credit terms;
- Make sure what you buy is of the right quality, and delivered on time;
- Ensure that full advantage is taken of any available credit;
- Pay the supplier the correct amount at the correct time;
- Protect the business's financial resources and avoid losses due to fraud and error;
- Avoid over-reliance on specific suppliers, where possible;
- Comply with the law, including tax laws; and

- Record and report the transactions accurately, promptly and efficiently.

These should be your main objectives where purchasing activities are concerned.

Cash vs credit purchases

Just like with sales (but in reverse!), your business might buy some things on credit, and it might also buy some things and pay for them straight away. And when it pays suppliers, it might pay straight from the business's bank account, it might pay from the owner's personal funds, or it might pay out of the business's cash funds. You'll need procedures to deal with all these aspects.

Keeping records

Whenever your business makes a purchase, you really must keep some sort of documentary evidence that the purchase happened. Usually this will be in the form of an invoice from the supplier. This is important for two reasons – firstly, for your record-keeping purposes, and secondly, to evidence that the transaction happened, because if HMRC launch an enquiry, they will expect to see documentary evidence to support the expenses your business incurred.

Developing that idea a bit further, you also need a system to capture and summarise your purchases. Ideally, you want to use some form of accountancy software, since that will make the whole process a lot easier. Modern cloud software like Quickbooks and Xero can even store electronic copies of your invoices, so that you don't have to keep the paper versions at all. Read more about accounting software at www.scholesca.co.uk/software.

Whether you use software, an excel spreadsheet or just a plain handwritten cashbook, there is a number of things you need to record, including:

- The name of the supplier;
- The date of purchase;
- The nature of the goods or services acquired;
- The cost of the supply;
- When the supplier was paid (if this differs from the date of purchase); and
- How the supplier was paid – in other words, were they paid from the business bank account, from the business's cash funds, or from the owner's own personal funds.

If your business is VAT registered, you will also need to record the net (i.e. VAT exclusive) cost, the VAT charged, and the gross (i.e. VAT inclusive) cost, and you may need to store all the details digitally (so handwritten records are definitely out).

Ideally you want your records to show clearly how much your business is spending across different *categories* of expenditure, so if you are using an excel spreadsheet or handwritten book, consider using different columns for different types of expenditure. This helps you see more easily how much your business is spending on different kinds of things.

How you decide what categories to use is really up to you, but some common ones might include: purchases for resale; rent & rates; heat & light; insurance; wages (we'll get to payroll soon); plant & equipment; postage & stationery; advertising; professional fees; bank charges; bank loan repayments. It really depends on what your business does.

If you're using accounting software to record your purchases, we'll talk about categorising expenditure using the "chart of accounts" a little later on.

Having considered some of the basics, let's now get into some of the broader financial processes associated with purchasing activities.

Budgeting

Before making a purchase, generally you'll need a clear idea that the business can afford to pay for it, and you'll want to make sure that the person committing the business to make the purchase (if it's not you) has the authority to do so!

We'll return to the subject of budgeting later on in this chapter. If there are people in the business who have the authority to make purchases (other than you as the business owner), do make sure the extent of that authority is clearly understood and communicated.

Selecting suppliers

Depending on the nature of the goods or services you're buying, you may need to consider how you go about selecting a supplier. Consider not just the price, but also, for example:

- The quality of the product or service;
- The timeliness and manner of delivery;
- The payment terms – how much credit will they grant you;
- The policy for returns (if goods are unsatisfactory or unsuitable);
- The quality of after-sales service; and
- Whether there are any issues with over-reliance on a specific supplier (what would happen if they stopped supplying your business?).

Even if you are happy with existing suppliers, consider also keeping them under review and "testing" alternative suppliers periodically to ensure you continue to enjoy the best deals.

Negotiating credit

In relation to significant orders, consider whether you are in a position to negotiate the terms of any credit on offer, since better credit terms from suppliers will help your business's cash flow. We return to the subject of cash flow in a later chapter – it is one of the most important things that you, as a business owner, need to be thinking about.

The purchase ordering process

Depending on the scale of your business and the number of people involved, you may need to implement a formal "purchase ordering" process. There are, potentially, several steps in the chain:

- A need to make a purchase is identified (for example, to replenish stock or replace some equipment);

- A "purchase order" is produced – this is a document requesting that the business should make the purchase;

- The purchase order is reviewed by someone else and approved (or modified or rejected!), having regard to the need for the order and any budgetary constraints;

- The approved orders are then executed (i.e. someone contacts one of the business's approved suppliers and orders the goods/ services);

- When the goods or services are subsequently received, they may be checked at the point of receipt against the purchase order to make sure they match whatever was ordered on specification, quality and quantity; and

- Goods received may be recorded on a "goods received note" and, if they are stocks bought for resale or further processing, they will also normally be recorded on the business's stock system at that point too (more on stock later).

To reduce the risk of financial losses arising from fraud or error, each role should be segregated as far as possible (unless you as the business owner are doing it all).

Paying suppliers

For all purchases made on credit, you'll need a system to pay suppliers. Depending on the scale of your business, this might include some or all of the following steps:

- Receiving supplier invoices and checking them against the goods received (this is one reason a "goods received note" is handy in some circumstances);
- Approving supplier invoices for payment;
- Recording supplier invoices in the business's accounting system;
- Paying the supplier invoice; and
- Recording the payment in the accounting records.

Again, unless you as the business owner are doing all of these things, segregating each role is strongly advisable to reduce the risk of fraud and error. If supplier payments are made through the business bank account then the ability to pay any third party *should* be limited to those individuals within your business who hold a mandate with the bank.

If some supplier payments are made out of the business's cash funds – if the business has cash funds e.g. as a retailer – then the scope for unapproved payments is potentially much wider. This is one reason why if your business holds significant funds in cash, regular reconciliations are critical, as discussed in the chapter on the sales process.

Monitoring outstanding creditors

If you use accounting software to record your purchases, it should be possible to produce and review an "aged creditors" report periodically. This is just like the aged debtors report described earlier, only it shows amounts due to be paid to suppliers, rather than amounts due to be collected from customers.

You'll want to review your aged creditors report periodically for a number of reasons. What are you looking for? If you employ staff who are responsible for aspects of the purchasing process, one thing you need to look out for is any suppliers on the report who are unfamiliar, as this may reveal unauthorised purchasing activity (or even fraud). Beyond that, you are really just looking at the report to identify what is owed to whom, and to enquire further into anything that appears overdue or unexpected for any reason.

If you receive statements of account from your suppliers, it's good practice to reconcile (i.e. match) the statement balance to the balance shown on your aged creditors report as any discrepancies may reveal a problem, such as a missing purchase invoice or payment error.

5

The expense claim process

Explaining the expense claim process

If you or your staff pay business expenses out of your own funds, and then reclaim them from the business, then you'll have an expense claim process. The main steps are usually:

- Agreeing what business expenses may be reclaimed from the business;
- Receiving expense claims from employees (normally in a prescribed format);
- Reviewing and approving expense claims;
- Paying the employee;

- Making and keeping a record of the transactions; and
- Reporting the transactions.

Claims may include not just expenses paid by the individual but also other allowances, e.g. mileage allowances, overnight incidentals etc.

Aims of the expense claim process

The main aims of the expense claim process from a financial perspective are to:

- Establish clearly the form and amount of costs that employees are entitled to reclaim from the business;
- Reimburse employees accurately and on a timely basis for expenses validly incurred;
- Protect the business's financial resources and avoid losses due to fraud and error;
- Comply with the law, including tax laws; and
- Record and report the transactions accurately, promptly and efficiently.

Is it necessary to have an expense claim process?

Perhaps the first thing to say is that dealing with expense claims involves more administration, so consider whether it is possible for the business to pay for all business transactions in the first instance, which then avoids the need for you (or your staff) to have to pay for and reclaim expenses. If you run a company, a company credit card can be a help here - but consider very carefully who in the business you are happy to provide a credit card to, for obvious reasons!

If you decide to pay for things personally and then reclaim those expenses from time to time, you should operate a system to capture and record the expenses that need to be reclaimed. This can be done using traditional methods (such as a spreadsheet) or you can do it using modern methods; there are loads of expense recording apps available to download to your smartphone, great for capturing images of taxi receipts, hotel bills etc.

Evidence will still need to be kept of the expenses incurred, i.e. paper or electronic copies of the invoices/ expense receipts – simply keeping a record of the claim, without the underlying documents, will not meet HMRC's requirements.

Periodically you (or your staff) can then total up the expense claim summary and have the business pay whatever is due. The payment can be entered into the accounting records, split as appropriate between different cost categories (travel, subsistence, postage & stationery, or whatever).

If your business is VAT registered, the VAT will also need to be recorded. It's generally permissible for a VAT registered business to reclaim the VAT on an invoice made out to an employee if the cost was incurred for business purposes – business travel, subsistence and accommodation costs or office supplies, for example (special rules apply in relation to VAT on motoring costs).

If you have employees who want to make expense claims, you (or someone) should review those claims before they are paid out, since expense claims is an area that can be very susceptible to fraud. Again, I'm not questioning the integrity of your staff – just thinking of the legions of frauds that I've read about over the years that involved employees manipulating, or even submitting entirely fictitious, expense claims. Don't let it happen to you!

6

The payroll process

Next we turn to payroll. If you employ staff (including yourself, if your business is run as a company), there are various processes you need to be concerned with.

Explaining the payroll process

The payroll process is concerned with various aspects of paying staff, and dealing with associated taxes and other deductions. For obvious reasons, you want to get it right - all the time, every time. Steps in the payroll process normally include:

- Agreeing and recording pay, terms and conditions for each employee;

- Monitoring tax and other legal and regulatory requirements that concern employers and employees;

- Monitoring staff attendance, sickness, overtime, and other elements that may affect what they are due to be paid;
- Calculating what employees are due to be paid, and what deductions need to be made (for example income tax and NIC, pensions, student loans) – including in relation to starters and leavers;
- Identifying and calculating any other statutory entitlements, e.g. sickness pay, maternity and paternity pay;
- Paying staff, HMRC and other agencies amounts due;
- Providing payslips to staff;
- Providing electronic payment submissions to HMRC;
- Making and keeping a record of the transactions; and
- Reporting the transactions.

The aims of the payroll process

The payroll process normally has several aims. You're looking to:

- Pay staff the correct amounts falling due under the terms of their employment;
- Pay HMRC the correct amounts due in law;

- Comply with broader legal and regulatory requirements (e.g. national minimum wage, workings hours directives and the like);
- Comply with tax reporting requirements;
- Protect the business's financial resources and avoid losses due to fraud and error; and
- Record and report the transactions accurately, promptly and efficiently.

Starters and leavers

In relation to starters, you'll need to decide what terms and conditions to offer; from a financial perspective this will include the rates of pay; entitlement to overtime; entitlement to holiday and sick pay; pension contributions; other benefits and expenses; and any contributions to training expenses.

In relation to leavers, there will be various financial considerations including working out pay due in the final period of service; dealing with notice periods and any payment in lieu of notice; and paying accrued holiday pay.

Employing staff is an area that is quite heavily regulated; there are rules about the national minimum wage; pension contributions that employers must make for employees; maximum working hours; sick pay, maternity and paternity pay; notice periods; insurance; health & safety; and much else besides. New staff must be given a written statement of the terms of employment.

It is therefore strongly advisable to take professional advice when considering taking on employees. E:mail me at ivan@scholesca.co.uk for further details.

Monitoring staff working time, absences, holidays

Having established the terms & conditions of employment, your business then needs to monitor what its employees are doing, to ensure they are complying with the terms of employment and, just as importantly, to ensure that your business complies fully with its obligations to the employees.

Consider what steps you need to take to track employee attendance, absences, holidays and similar.

Going one step further, if your staff are engaged in productive activities (such as delivering a service to customers or making products for resale), you are likely to need a timesheet system to record how much time they spend on different activities. A timesheet system will also be needed if your employees get paid extra for working overtime.

A record of staff time will help you work out what it is costing your business to make and supply goods or services to customers, and you need to know this so you can price your products and services correctly and understand how much money the business is making (or losing).

Processing payroll and dealing with income tax, NIC, pensions and other deductions

Unless all your staff earn under the NIC threshold and have no other employment, your business will need to operate formal payroll and PAYE procedures. This means that, each time staff are paid, it needs to work out what income tax and NIC needs to be deducted from the wages and paid over to HMRC.

Payroll details must be submitted to HMRC electronically whenever staff are paid, and any tax and NIC must be paid by the business to HMRC by 22nd falling immediately after the end of the tax month (tax months end on the 5th of each month).

Your business may also be obliged to make pension contributions on behalf of its employees, and make various other deductions such as student loan repayments.

Employees should be given a payslip when they are paid setting out their pay before and after any deductions, and setting out details of the amounts deducted. Nowadays payslips may be provided in paper or electronic format. There are additional reporting requirements in relation to the tax year as a whole.

If your payroll is very simple, you may be tempted to do it all yourself using HMRC's Basic Tools (available online). Alternatively, there are various payroll software packages on the market, and these are generally fine to use as long as you are familiar with all the rules.

For many businesses it is advisable to outsource all the payroll processing to a third party such as an experienced accountant, who will generally be able to do the job accurately and at reasonable cost.

Paying employees and HMRC

As well as running the payroll, you'll also need to ensure that your staff and HMRC get paid on time.

The amount of the payments should be determined by reference to the payroll – staff should be paid amounts net of any deductions; HMRC should be paid the total due for the tax month.

Most businesses pay staff electronically these days (by BACS or similar). If you really *must* pay your staff in cash, then if at all possible have two people involved – one to count up the cash, the other to recount it and match it to the net amount due per the payslip. It helps avoid mistakes and disputes.

Recording payroll transactions in the accounting records

The amounts payable to staff, HMRC and other bodies will all need to be recorded in your accounting records – as will the actual payments.

If you are using accounting software such as Quickbooks Online, Xero, or Sage, then you should enter the amounts payable using the data from your payroll. If your payroll and accounting systems are linked, you may even be able to automate this step, which is great as it will save you time and reduce the likelihood of errors. When the payments are made, they should be entered into the correct account in your software – wages payable; PAYE/ NIC payable; or pensions payable.

Entering the amounts payable, as well as the actual payments, helps ensure that i) your accounting software shows the true cost of employing staff, because it will include all costs that have been incurred, not just those already paid; and ii) any discrepancies between what was supposed to be paid and what was actually paid (to staff, HMRC, or the pension scheme) are more readily identifiable.

If you are keeping a very simple cashbook system then just record the actual payments as they are made.

Unless you are responsible for all aspects of payroll, it is strongly advisable to segregate the roles of processing the payroll, making the payments, and entering the transactions into your accounting system.

Reconciling the wages and PAYE control accounts

If you operate accounting software and enter amounts *payable* per the payroll (as well as the amounts actually *paid*), this provides the opportunity to check that the correct amounts have been paid using "control accounts".

It works like this. When you enter the amounts *payable* into your accounting software, this creates both a cost (because wages are an expense) and a liability – an amount payable by the business (because the business has to pay someone – the employee, HMRC etc.). Those liabilities sit in control accounts – there is a control account for wages due to staff, one for PAYE due to HMRC, one for any pension contributions due to the pension scheme, and so on.

When you actually pay the staff, HMRC etc, the payments should be entered into the relevant control account. So the value of the liability in each control account goes up whenever a payroll is run; and goes back down when the amounts payable are actually paid.

Here's the point: by looking at the amounts in the control accounts at any point in time, and the running balance (amounts payable less amounts actually paid) it should be possible to tell whether the business is up to date and has made all the payments due correctly. The balance on any of the control accounts should usually be just the very latest amounts due per the payroll – or nil (if the latest amounts due have already been paid).

Control accounts are often used by bookkeepers and accountants to monitor and check various areas of a business's accounts; the wages and PAYE control accounts are common examples but there are many others.

Later on in the book we look at the subject of employing staff in slightly more detail.

7

The construction industry scheme

If your business operates in the construction industry, you may choose to, or have to, register for the construction industry scheme (CIS for short).

Contractors – businesses that pay subcontractors for construction work – must:

- Register for CIS;
- Withhold income tax from payments made to subcontractors for their labour;
- Keep detailed records of the tax withheld;
- Provide the subcontractors with "payment and deduction statements" showing the tax withheld;

- Account for the tax withheld to HMRC on monthly returns that have to be submitted by the 19th, 14 days after the end of the month (CIS reporting periods are the same as for PAYE, 6th to the 5th of each month);

- Pay to HMRC the tax withheld, by the 22nd of the month (assuming the payments are made electronically rather than by cheque).

Subcontractors do not have to register for CIS but it is normally advantageous to do so because contractors will withhold tax at a rate of 30% when paying subcontractors who are not CIS registered, but at a rate of only 20% when paying subcontractors who are registered.

If your construction business trades as a sole trade or partnership, then any tax withheld by your customers will normally be entered in your Self Assessment return where it is offset against your income tax liability.

If your construction business trades as a limited company, then any tax withheld by your customers will normally be offset against the company's monthly PAYE liabilities.

Subcontractors who are CIS registered may apply to HMRC for "gross payment status", if awarded this status then they can be paid by contractors with no deduction at all. Gross payment status is normally awarded only to subcontractors who can demonstrate a good track record of managing and paying their taxes on time, and who are of reasonable scale.

Attaining gross payment status can offer big cash flow advantages so should generally be pursued wherever possible.

8

Banking processes

We've already touched on the subject of dealing with receipts and payments earlier in this chapter, in the context of sales, purchases, and payroll. Let's get into the subject in a bit more detail now; there are various banking processes happening in most small businesses.

Explaining banking processes

Key steps within the banking processes may include:

- Opening bank accounts;
- Determining who within the business has the authority to access the bank account or make payments;
- Banking cash and cheques received by the business;

- Making payments from the bank account/ transferring money between accounts;
- Making and keeping a record of the transactions; and
- Reporting the transactions.

Aims of banking processes

Banking processes have several objectives. You will want to:

- Ensure that receipts are banked to the correct account on a timely basis;
- Ensure that payments are made accurately;
- Prevent unauthorised payments;
- Ensure that the company's bank accounts are protected from unauthorised activity;
- Protect the business's financial resources and avoid losses due to fraud and error; and
- Record and report the transactions accurately, promptly and efficiently.

No matter the size of your business, you need to get your banking processes right from day one as these form the beating heart of the financial system in just about any organisation. Get it right, and you will have established a fair degree of control over what is going on in your business; get it wrong, and you'll probably have no idea what is going on, and you may be much more susceptible to financial losses through fraud and simple error. The choice is yours!

Business vs personal

Wherever possible, your business should operate its own bank account rather than using personal bank accounts for business purposes – or vice-versa. If your business is a company this is really a given, if you're a sole trader or in partnership, maybe not so much.

Anyway, the message is simple: keep your personal and business transactions entirely separate and don't mix the two – just don't do it. If you really *must*, you'll probably find it much harder to track what's going on in your business, and your accountant will have a tough job disentangling everything at the end of each financial year (and you'll pay for it with a fee that reflects all the extra work they have to do!).

Bank reconciliation

As we've already seen, whether or not you use accounting software, you should have some system to record all the income your business receives, and all the payments that it makes (including payroll and expense claims). How can you make sure that you've recorded everything completely and correctly? How can you spot any unauthorised activity involving your business bank account? That's where a bank reconciliation helps.

The humble bank reconciliation: dear to every accountant's heart; much maligned and misunderstood; often poorly performed by the untrained; but absolutely important and necessary and fundamental to making sure your accounting records are accurate.

What is a bank reconciliation? It's what you do when you check the bank balance and transactions *as recorded in your accounting records* to the bank balance and transactions *as recorded in the bank statements*.

The point of the exercise is simply to prove (to yourself, and anyone else who cares) that the payments and receipts you have recorded in your accounting software (or on your spreadsheet, or wherever you happen to record them) are accurately and completely stated. That is the simple but very important point of a bank reconciliation.

Here's the *real* point: if you don't reconcile your business bank account from time to time, then any mistakes you have made in recording your business's payments and receipts will quite possibly go undetected. Consequently, your records may be riddled with errors, and as a result you may end up making bad decisions, committing further mistakes, failing to comply with obligations to the tax authorities, lenders, and suppliers, failing to collect all monies due from customers, and so on. And on and on. Bank reconciliations are important, you see!

What about if you use cloud accounting software that 'pulls in' all your bank transactions direct from your bank account? Is a bank reconciliation still necessary? I would argue that it is, for three reasons:

1. The software is not always 100% reliable so it may fail to pull in all the transactions automatically;

2. If your business still writes cheques, your software won't enter those payments with the payment date, only the date the cheque cleared the bank, but for year-end accounting purposes it is the payment date (not the date on the bank statement) that counts; and

3. Actually checking the bank balance and comparing it to the balance on your accounting software is still the only way to know *for sure* that your software is showing a complete record of all transactions and is not carrying any historic errors.

If you can give your accountant a bank reconciliation as at your business's financial year-end this will reduce the work they have to do and it might even save you a few quid off your accountancy fee. I'm talking from experience here!

Selecting a banking provider

For a new business (or the owner of an existing business who has had enough of their current bank!), selecting a banking partner merits some careful thought.

If you're a sole trader, then it's possible just to use an existing personal bank account, and this can save on bank charges, but you really want to keep the business and personal transactions going through separate accounts if at all possible.

If you're operating a partnership (i.e. the business is you plus one or more partners sharing in the decision making and sharing the profits (or losses!)) then you'll really need a bank account in the name of the partnership.

If you're operating a company, you'll definitely need a bank account in the company's name, no question.

Speaking frankly, in my experience there really isn't much to differentiate the main high street banks generally, so if you want to open an account for your business and you already have a relationship with a particular bank and you are not wildly dissatisfied with the service, you could start there. At least you may not have to show them passports, utility bills and other evidence to prove you are you.

All the textbooks will say that when comparing banks you should compare the charges, interest rates, arrangement fees and so on, which is all good common sense, I suppose. What may be of most value, though, is finding a bank that is easy to do business with, on a practical level. Do they have a local branch? Even better, do they have a local business manager who will give you their time, rather than just directing you to some distant call centre? And, if you need to borrow, will they lend you money on sensible terms?

Setting up the mandate

As well as opening a bank account, you may need to think carefully about who (other than yourself) will have access i) to see the bank transactions and, even more importantly, ii) to make payments.

If the business is run by you and you have no partners or staff, the decision may be abundantly clear. If, however, you have a business partner, a co-director, or a trusted member of staff, it may be desirable, or essential, to extend the mandate to include them too.

You just need to strike the right balance, ensuring that the business can operate efficiently in your absence, without compromising financial control. If you are out of the country or incapacitated, how will the business pay its bills or its staff? If your bookkeeper has the authority to initiate BACS payments (or sign cheques), how will you ensure that the payments they initiate are made only for legitimate reasons, to the correct accounts, for the correct amounts?

With online banking systems it is usually possible to impose daily/aggregate limits on the amounts that can be paid without your prior approval so that's a good place to start. With online banking you can also normally control who can set up or change supplier bank accounts, another useful way to limit the potential for unauthorised activity.

9

Tax compliance processes

You will need appropriate processes to help fulfil your business's obligations to submit information to the tax authorities and pay any taxes as they fall due. This is because UK businesses are required to comply with UK laws, including tax laws, and failing to do so can result in severe financial penalties and censure of the directors/proprietors.

The main taxes we are generally concerned with here are: VAT; PAYE; and corporation tax. If you are trading as a sole trader or as a partner in a partnership, then income tax will be an important consideration for you personally, but since income tax is a personal tax and not a business tax, it's really outside the scope of this book so I won't cover it further here. Maybe that'll be the next book. Anyway, moving on...

VAT

If your business is VAT registered, you will need to prepare, review, and submit VAT returns to HMRC on a quarterly or monthly basis. Returns are due by the 7th of the month following the month after the period end (so for example the return for a period ending 31st March will be due no later than 7th May).

Quarterly reporting is the default position but many businesses, especially those that tend to be due a repayment from HMRC, submit monthly returns instead.

VAT returns are usually generated using accounting software, based on the transaction details that have been entered into the software for the period in question.

For the most part, VAT returns are now submitted "digitally", meaning that the accounting software interfaces with HMRC's systems and the VAT return data transfers across that interface via controls within the accounting software.

You will also need to ensure that the payment is made to HMRC on time (or that the repayment is received from HMRC within a reasonable timeframe, where applicable), and that the payment (or receipt) is recorded in your accounting system. The due date for payment is the same as the due date for the return.

Accounting software will include a "VAT control account" where amounts due to and from HMRC are recorded. The control account should be checked periodically to confirm that the transactions are correctly stated.

We'll get more into VAT later in this book.

Payroll

We've already discussed the payroll process. To summarise, each payroll needs to be prepared, reviewed, and submitted to HMRC electronically, on (or before) payday. Amounts due to HMRC for PAYE/ NIC need to be paid on time. Staff need to be given payslips, and they also need to be paid on time. The transactions all need to be recorded in your accounting records correctly and promptly. And your "PAYE control account" should be checked periodically to confirm that the transactions are correctly stated and identify any problems with under/ overpayments.

Normally PAYE payments are due to be made no later than 22nd immediately following the end of the PAYE period, and PAYE reporting periods are usually monthly, running from 6th of one month to 5th of the next month. So for example the PAYE for the period ended 5th May will be due for payment no later than 22nd May.

Some businesses with quite a small payroll may instead pay PAYE to HMRC on quarterly basis, which helps cash flow. E:mail me at ivan@scholesca.co.uk for details.

Corporation tax

If your business trades as a company, it will be liable to pay corporation tax which is a tax on profits and gains the company makes in the course of its activities.

As far as small companies are concerned, corporation tax falls due for payment nine months and one day after the end of the "accounting period". Usually (but not always) the "accounting period" for this purpose means the period for which the company draws up formal accounts. So for example a company which draws up accounts for the year ended 31st March 2019 will have to pay any corporation tax due in respect of that year by 1st January 2020.

Weirdly, although the tax is due for payment nine months and one day after the end of the period, the actual return can be submitted up to twelve months after the company's financial year end, without penalty. In the above example the return is due no later than 31st March 2020 – even though any tax must be paid by 1st January 2020. Don't ask me why – that's just what the rules say!

Companies with very high profits have to pay corporation tax in quarterly instalments but that's unlikely to apply to the businesses run by most readers of this book!

Anyway, as far as the process is concerned, someone needs to prepare, review, and submit the corporation tax returns; make the payments (or recover any repayments) on time; and record all the transactions on your accounting system.

Usually the job of preparing and submitting corporation tax returns is handled by an accountant, but the business owner should definitely maintain a keen interest in all aspects of the process, not least because this might present the opportunity to identify ways to save tax in future. And in law, the responsibility for complying with the tax rules always rests ultimately with the business/ business owner – not with the business's advisers.

10

Fixed asset management processes

Fixed assets, basically, are the things your business owns that are used to help run the business and generate an income. They come in three flavours: tangible assets (things you can see and touch, like a building, plant & machinery, office equipment or vehicles); intangible assets (things you can't touch, like computer software or patents); and investments (like shares in other companies).

You'll need procedures to help you manage and control your business's fixed assets. Let's have a look at those procedures now.

Explaining the fixed asset management process

Managing your business's fixed assets may involve a number of important steps. Focusing on tangible assets (since these are by far the most common form of fixed assets held by small businesses), important steps may include:

- Identifying requirements to acquire fixed assets;
- Scoping out the requirements in detail and confirming that funds (or finance) are available;
- Selecting a supplier;
- Buying the assets (see purchases process);
- Repairing & maintaining fixed assets;
- Protecting the physical security of assets held;
- Performing periodic checks of assets back to the fixed asset register, and vice-versa;
- Identifying assets to be sold or scrapped;
- Selling or exchanging fixed assets at the end of their useful life (see sales process);
- Maintaining an inventory of assets acquired, held, disposed;
- Estimating how quickly the assets are being used up ("depreciation");
- Making and keeping a record of the transactions; and
- Reporting the transactions.

Aims of the fixed asset management process

Since fixed assets are an important component of many small businesses, the fixed asset management process seeks to accomplish a number of objectives. Here you are looking to:

- Ensure that any expenditure commitments are within the business's financial capacity;
- Prevent unauthorised expenditure;
- Buy the best available for the budget;
- Protect the physical security of the assets;
- Promptly identify and repair or dispose of any assets that are impaired or obsolete;
- Protect the business's financial resources and avoid losses due to fraud and error; and
- Record and report the transactions accurately, promptly and efficiently.

Buying and selling fixed assets

If you're the only one working in the business, this one's a doddle: you decide what you need to buy and sell and that's that. There are, of course, important considerations about whether and when to buy or sell assets, and whether it makes economic sense to do so — that's where budgeting and planning becomes relevant, and we'll get into that later on.

If you have fellow directors, business partners, or staff, then the position is a bit more complicated as you'll need to decide who

Fixed asset management processes

within the business has the authority to buy (and sell) fixed assets. This is important because a when it comes to fixed assets we are often talking about significant amounts of money and the income-generating potential they represent. So be clear on who in your business has the authority to buy or sell fixed assets.

Maintaining a fixed asset register

If your business possesses any significant fixed assets, a register of those assets should be maintained. The register should list out the specific assets held, the date of acquisition, the acquisition cost (and any subsequent enhancement cost), and the amount of "depreciation" charged to date. If you'd like a free fixed asset register template, e:mail me at ivan@scholesca.co.uk.

Depreciation, by the way, is just an accountant's term for estimating how a fixed asset is "used up" over successive financial periods – a monetary value is determined, based on an estimate of how long an asset might be used for and what value (if any) the asset might have when the business will stop using it, and that value, the "depreciation charge" is shown as a cost in the profit & loss account each year the asset is used by the business. The value of the asset for accounting purposes - the "net book value" of the asset – is reduced each year by the depreciation charge.

Anyway, a register of your business's fixed assets needs to be maintained, and periodically checks should be performed between the register, your accounting records, and the actual assets (as seen on the shop floor - or wherever you happen to keep them):

- To make sure that the assets listed on the register and in your accounting system are still in your possession (and to follow up if anything seems to have gone missing);
- To make sure that the register and your accounts accurately reflect all the assets that your business currently holds (and to update/ correct them if they contain errors); and
- To identify any assets whose condition suggests they may be overvalued in the accounts/ register, so you can then adjust the depreciation charges as needed.

Recording sales and purchases and depreciation charges

The depreciation charges should be entered into your accounting system on a monthly or quarterly basis using "journal entries". We'll come back to journal entries shortly.

Where fixed assets are scrapped – disposed of for no money - entries will still need to be made in your accounting system to show that your business now longer owns the assets, and to write off any of the original cost that has not already been written off through depreciation. Again this is done using journal entries.

As with all other purchase and sales transactions, the purchase or sale of assets, and the associated payment or receipt, need to be entered into your accounting system accurately and on a timely basis.

Once again, unless you're doing all the bookkeeping, you'll want to segregate the roles of buying and selling assets, dealing with the payments/ receipts, entering the transactions into your accounting system, and maintaining the fixed asset register — at least as far as possible.

11

Stock management processes

If your business sells goods (not just services) then you'll need processes to manage your stock, especially if the stock is valuable.

This is even more important if your business doesn't just buy and sell things but *makes or transforms* things, because you'll need to be able to work out what it's costing you to make the finished product, so you'll need to be able to identify not just the cost of the raw materials, but also your labour costs, any subcontracted labour costs, any items "consumed" in the production process, and, potentially, a proportion of overheads, too.

Explaining stock management processes

Stock management processes typically include various steps, here are some common examples:

- Monitoring stock levels to ensure that optimum amounts of stock are being held;
- Identifying any requirements to re-order stock (either finished goods or raw materials);
- Ordering stock and booking it in on receipt (see purchases process);
- Producing the finished goods ready for sale;
- Monitoring and recording the costs of purchase and production;
- Despatching goods and booking them out (see sales process);
- Monitoring and maintaining the physical security of stocks held;
- Maintaining accurate records of stocks held, including any stocks held by third parties; and
- Performing periodic checks of stock back to the stock records, and vice-versa.

Aims of the stock management process

In managing your stock you are aiming to:

- Maintain accurate records of all stock movements;

- Hold the optimum quantity of stock at all times – avoiding stock-outs and not overstocking;
- Protect the physical security of all stocks held;
- Promote the security of any stock held at third party locations, or in transit;
- Promptly identify any slow-moving, damaged or obsolete stock;
- Protect the business's financial resources and avoid losses due to fraud and error; and
- Record and report the quantity and value of stock held accurately, promptly and efficiently.

Real time stock systems

Some businesses maintain a "real time" stock system (or "job costing system") that is meant to continuously show the quantity, cost and selling price of stocks held at any point in time. This is a good idea (often absolutely essential) for certain types of business, including those:

- With significant stock;
- That manufacture goods;
- That have complicated or extended production processes (think: construction); and
- With high volumes of transactions (think: retail/ wholesale).

Other businesses don't maintain a live stock system but perform periodic assessments of the cost and quantity of stock held at specific points in the year; in very small businesses this may be done only once a year, at the financial year-end. Whether or not your business should operate a live stock system will depend very much on the nature and scale of what it does.

Keeping stock records up to date

We've already spoken about the importance of recording when goods are bought or sold, in the context of the purchases and sales your business makes (remember those "goods received notes" and "goods despatched notes" we spoke about?).

In a live stock system, your purchases, sales and (if you manufacture) payroll transactions all become important "feeds" into the system. So you need to make sure your stock system is updated accurately for the movement of goods into and out of the business, and for any associated manufacturing costs. This may be done manually or, if you operate a stock system that is integrated with your accounting system, it may be possible to automate some of the process.

Generally, stocks should be valued, for financial management and accounting purposes, at their cost to bring them into their current location and condition. Cost will exclude any VAT, if the business is VAT registered and able to reclaim the VAT from HMRC.

The exception is where their "net realisable value" (basically what they are likely to sell for, less any costs necessary to complete and sell them) is less than their cost – in that case we value them at their "net realisable value". This is the fabled "lower of cost and net realisable value" rule. You don't want to value stock at its estimated selling price, because if you were to do this, your profit & loss account would show a profit that your business has not (yet) made!

So whether your business maintains a live stock system or just performs periodic stock counts, you need to be able to determine:

- The quantities and cost of each stock type;
- The cost to the business of bringing the stock into its current location and condition (including manufacturing costs, if applicable); and
- The estimated selling price of the stock (less an estimate of any costs to complete and sell it).

Stock counts

Stock counts should be performed periodically - even if you operate a live stock system - because they provide assurance that your business does indeed hold the stock you expect it to hold!

It is really only by actually counting and checking the condition of the stock, and comparing it to your stock records – and vice-versa – that you can definitively:

- Confirm that the financial records accurately reflect the quantities and appropriate values of stock;
- Identify any missing items for further investigation; and

- Identify slow-moving, damaged or obsolete stock items that may need to be written-down (or written off) in your accounting and stock records – and recycled or sold for scrap.

For any business holding significant stock, the absolute bare minimum frequency of physical stock counts is annually, on the financial year-end date.

Stock counts have to be performed carefully to avoid double-counting or missing items, and you'll also need procedures to identify and deal with any items held at third-party locations; any goods in transit; and associated "cut off" issues (for example where a customer has been invoiced for stock but the stock is still sitting in your warehouse, or where a supplier has invoiced you for raw materials but those raw materials have not yet been received). Proceed with care...

12

Nominal ledger processes

Don't be scared by the term "nominal ledger" – it basically just means the place where your business's transactions are all recorded!

In the old days the nominal ledger was a paper book – literally a ledger (there was also a separate sales ledger, for sales, and a purchase ledger, for purchases). Nowadays these "ledgers" are nearly always kept digitally; if you use (or plan to use) accounting software, you'll be using a nominal ledger (whether you know it or not!).

We'll talk more about accounting software a bit later on, but for now we'll cover a few basic points.

Explaining nominal ledger processes

If you use accounting software, you'll probably undertake most (if not all) the following steps:

- Setting up and maintaining a chart of accounts (explained below);
- Entering transactions into the ledger – e.g. sales, purchases, payroll, bank payments and receipts;
- Entering journals into the ledger (also explained below);
- Checking and reconciling data that has been entered into the ledger; and
- Backing up the data periodically.

Aims of nominal ledger processes

The nominal ledger is the place where all your business's transactional data comes together. Here you're seeking to:

- Maintain an accurate record of the business's financial transactions and overall financial performance and position;
- Keep all transactional data safe and secure;
- Prevent unauthorised access to the data; and
- Establish the foundation for accurate financial reporting and decision-making.

The chart of accounts

It's important to appreciate that any time a transaction is entered into accounting software – whether we are talking about a sale, a purchase, a bank payment or receipt, a tax payment, a bank loan, or a dividend payment – literally *any* transaction, in fact – it needs to be classified in the software.

Transactions are classified according to their type – they may represent income or expenses, assets (things the business owns) or liabilities (things the business owes), or investor's capital - so we need a way to differentiate between the different types of transaction your business will need to record in the nominal ledger. We do this using a series of "nominal accounts" that are contained within the accounting software.

Your accounting software should be set up to contain a whole series of "nominal accounts" – these are just separate records, if you like, representing the various different kinds of asset, liability, income, expense, or capital. This series of nominal accounts is also known as the "chart of accounts".

You'll want to make sure the chart of accounts in your accounting software is set up in the best way for your business, bearing in mind the kinds of activities your business pursues and how it operates. Modern accounting software normally comes with a "default" chart of accounts, but ideally you should tailor it for your business's specific requirements.

Whenever a transaction is entered into your accounting software, the software will either prompt you to say which nominal account(s) the transaction relates to, or it will do it automatically. This is the point where the meaningful classification takes place, because the nominal account(s) the transaction is associated with determines where it will show up on your profit & loss account or balance sheet.

Transactions need to be posted to the correct nominal account(s) so that reports generated by your software – like the profit & loss account or balance sheet – give you an *accurate* idea about your business's financial performance and position. The same information may also be used to comply with tax and accounting reporting rules, and if the information used subsequently proves to be incorrect then there may be adverse consequences for the business.

Debits and credits

It's no accident that a balance sheet is called a balance sheet. In accountant world, there is a debit for every credit, and vice-versa.

All this really means is that any transaction your business undertakes always has *two* effects, and any transaction recorded in your accounting software will similarly have *two* effects. Examples:

- You sell some product and the customer pays money to your bank: your income goes up and your bank balance (an asset) goes up *by the same amount*

- You pay the supplier: your bank balance goes down and the amount payable to the supplier (a liability) goes down *by the same amount;*

Small business financial management

- You buy a new van and pay for it with money from the bank: your fixed assets go up and your bank balance goes down *by the same amount*;
- You receive a bank loan: your bank balance goes up and the amount payable to the bank (a liability) goes up *by the same amount.*

Back in the days when nominal ledgers were paper-based, any transaction would be entered in two different places, just like in the examples above. That's still the case today - every debit has a corresponding credit, and the debit(s) and credit(s) must both total the same amount:

DEBITS	CREDITS
Expenses	Income
Assets	Liabilities
	Owner's capital

Fortunately, with the advent of modern accounting software, most of this stuff now happens in the background, without users even being aware that it is happening.

The one place where it does still visibly happen is with "journal entries"...

Journals

Journals... the very word seems to fill most business owners (even some bookkeepers) with dread. Let me allay your fears.

If you use accounting software, the first thing to say here is that about 95% of your accounting entries can normally be made without going near a journal.

If you simply enter all your sales, purchases, payments and receipts correctly, on a timely basis, allocate them to the right nominal accounts, and apply VAT correctly (if your business is VAT registered), then most of the legwork is done already.

Journals usually come into play when we want to show things in the accounts that do not arise from, or relate to, the normal purchasing and selling routines. We can use journals to record, for example:

- The depreciation of fixed assets;
- Changes in the quantity and value of stocks (although if your stock and accounting systems are integrated, they may generate those journal entries automatically);

Small business financial management

- Income that has been earned but not (yet) invoiced or received;
- Prepaid and accrued expenses (to make sure that income and expenses appear in the appropriate financial period);
- Amounts due to employees and HMRC for payroll/ PAYE (although if your payroll and accounting systems are integrated, they may generate journals automatically);
- Costs that we know the business has incurred, that are not invoiced – e.g. liabilities due under asset finance arrangements, or corporation tax; and
- Estimates of expenses incurred, where the exact timing or amount may be unknown – we call these "provisions".

Journals are usually entered on the last day of the reporting period – so that might be monthly, quarterly, or annually, depending on how frequently you wish to produce and use financial reports.

When entering any journal, there will always be a minimum of two entries – at least one debit and at least one credit - and the total debits and total credits must always match. Good software won't let you post a journal that does not balance!

Maintaining the nominal ledger

Your nominal ledger – your accounting software – is very important, so it needs to be well maintained. You'll need to ensure that the data is recorded accurately, and on a timely basis.

To make sure your business's financial data is as accurate as possible, you should aim to review the transactions and balances shown in the software – in the ledger – periodically, by which I mean monthly (or at least quarterly). I've already touched on some of the reconciliations and checks that should be performed, including:

- Fixed assets - checking the fixed asset register back to the ledger;

- Stock - checking the stock values from your stock system (or stock count) back to the ledger;

- Bank reconciliations – checking the bank balance on the software to the bank statement;

- Reviewing aged debtors – reviewing the aged debtors report and checking anything that seems incorrect or overdue; checking the balance on aged debtors back to the balance on your balance sheet;

- Reviewing aged creditors – reviewing the aged creditors and, again, checking anything that seems untoward; checking the balance on aged creditors back to the balance on your balance sheet; and

- Reconciling other control accounts back to the underlying records – including PAYE and VAT.

Beyond that, you should also be producing management accounts (we'll get to that next!) – this is pretty easy if you've been keeping your records up to date – and reviewing them carefully. If you do this regularly, this will also help you confirm that the data in your accounting software is all up to date (as well as helping you manage your business's finances properly!).

What else do you need to do to maintain and look after your nominal ledger correctly? You'll need to control strictly who has access to it, using appropriate password controls. Similarly you'll want to make sure no one makes any unauthorised changes to the system or the data.

Protecting your data from loss due to theft, general carelessness, and natural catastrophes (e.g. fires and floods) is also a very good idea, so make sure you keep any hard drives or pen drives as secure as possible, and make regular backups that are not held at the same location (as that defeats the purpose of making a backup). Or, perhaps better still, use a cloud accounting product like Quickbooks Online or Xero, so that the whole business of keeping backups becomes someone else's problem.

13

The accounts production process

We've covered the basics – the day to day financial routines relating to your business's activities. If you grow your business (or if your business already has reasonable scale), perhaps you already employ staff who can do much of the day to day financial stuff for you, or maybe you outsource some of the activities to an accountant or bookkeeper.

The point where you as a business owner absolutely, unquestionably need to get interested – *regardless of who is doing everything else* – is the bit where you produce accounts from your accounting system. These accounts – we call them "management accounts" – should be produced regularly (ideally monthly) and you should review them carefully and in detail in order to figure out your business's *financial performance* (is it making a profit?) and its *financial position* (does it have the resources to pay its bills on time and keep trading?).

Unless you run an incredibly simple business, producing and reviewing management accounts is really the only way to *completely* understand how your business is doing, from a financial perspective.

Running a business without an accurate understanding of its financial performance and position is like driving a car without a steering wheel or mirrors – it probably won't end well. And that's why I devote part 2 of the book to understanding accounts.

14

Budgeting & forecasting processes

Whereas your management accounts are backward-looking – they tell you about the company's finances in the past – you also need to be able to plan ahead, to figure out what the finances might look like in the future. You need a budgeting process.

Businesses normally budget on an annual basis. A budget helps answer a number of questions, for example:

- What might the income, expenses, profit or loss be in future periods, and how might this be affected by different decisions I make?

- Will there be sufficient cash to enable bills to be paid as they fall due?

- What investments will my business need to make to achieve its objectives?
- What financial resources will my business need to meet its objectives?
- How much can I afford to pay myself/ my staff?
- What sort of return might investors in the business (shareholders) expect?
- Will my business need to raise money (for example by borrowing, using asset finance etc)?
- What might be the tax implications associated with the projected income and expenses?

Having agreed and communicated a budget, many businesses will then proceed to update it periodically through the year as events unfold – this is known as forecasting.

Budgeting & forecasting is a very important tool in your financial management armoury, so I return to it in more detail later in the book when we consider in depth how to use your accounts to manage your small business's finances.

15

Administration

Here are some other points to bear in mind, in relation to your basic financial processes.

Record keeping

You should keep your financial records at least seven years. The good news is you don't have to keep paper copies of most records – electronic copies of invoices and bank statements are fine. Just make sure they are backed up!

Documenting your financial processes and procedures

Your financial processes and procedures should be documented in the form of "how to" instructions, so that you (and, if applicable, your staff) know what needs to be done and when.

Documenting and communicating roles, responsibilities and authority levels

You should also document and communicate authority levels – who has authority to undertake specific activities. Some decisions and activities you will wish to make personally; others, you may be happy to delegate to your employees. Being clear about this from the outset will help avoid a whole bunch of problems "down the road".

16

Choosing accounting software

If you or your staff keep (or plan to keep) your business's day-to-day accounting records – rather than outsourcing all the work to a bookkeeper or accountant - then the chances are you will be using accounting software of one kind or another. A spreadsheet might be OK at the very beginning, but if you plan to grow your business, or if your business is going to be VAT registered, then proper accounting software really is the way to go.

These days, there are really two main options when it comes to selecting accounting software:

- *Desktop packages* such as Sage Accounts or Quickbooks; and

- *Cloud packages* such as Quickbooks Online, Xero, or Freeagent.

Desktop packages are the "traditional" form of accounting software. The software is run on a machine in your office, home, laptop etc, and the data is stored on your server or hard drive. Typically, the data is only accessible from the computer/ server on which it is stored.

Cloud packages are the "new" way to keep accounting data. The software is accessed on the internet, and your data is stored on a server somewhere far, far away, and looking after it is the responsibility of whichever cloud provider you've chosen to use.

Choosing between the two comes down to a careful consideration of various issues. Let's have a look at the pros and cons of each type of system.

Advantages of cloud accounting systems

Cloud accounting systems allow users to access their business financial data at any time from any location with internet access, this is obviously very useful if you like to work "on the go".

Cloud systems can generally link with the business's bank account and automatically feed in details of the business's receipts and payments. This can be a big time and money saver as it can remove the need for someone to type in each individual bank transaction.

Another benefit of the cloud approach is that there is a large "ecosystem" of software programmes – apps – that can be bolted on, so the cloud user can to some extent really "tailor" their accounting system to the specific needs of the business. There are apps for stock management, timesheets and holiday management, and forecasting and budgeting - to quote just a few examples.

If you are happy with technology and keen to reduce the "paper chase" involved in dealing with reams of invoices, cloud systems can also be used to capture and store images of invoices and other documents. In the right circumstances this enables users to operate more efficiently, reduce the need to organise and store loads of documents, and deal with things like expense claims more speedily.

When working with your accountant, having your data in the cloud can also be very helpful – I find that conversations with my clients are more constructive and productive when I can log onto their accounting system and see exactly how their business is doing, and I can even update or correct their data without having to mess about swapping pen drives or emailing backup data backwards and forwards.

With your accounting data stored in the cloud, the responsibility for keeping it safe and secure rests with the cloud service provider, which means you don't have to worry about backing it up locally.

Finally, cloud systems are generally cheaper to subscribe to, compared to the desktop equivalents. Most cloud accounting providers offer a range of "tiered" pricing options, with different levels of features in each package, depending on the needs of users.

Advantages of desktop accounting systems

Using a desktop accounting system, your financial data will be stored on your hard drive or server. This means you will be solely responsible for backing it up and preventing loss due to some unexpected event (fire, flood etc). Arguably this is an advantage over cloud based systems because you stay in control of the protection of your data.

If you are worried that storing and accessing your accounting data online would make it unacceptably vulnerable to hacking, then desktop accounting may be the answer. That said, the main cloud accounting outfits all claim that their data encryption routines are at least as secure as those of the high street banks – if not more so.

It would be fair to say that cloud systems are not necessarily suited to processing very high volumes of data, so if you need to process a lot of accounting transactions – in the tens of thousands annually – then this may point to using a desktop system.

Similarly, if your business has very complex accounting needs, this might again point towards a desktop based system. There are some bespoke desktop systems that have been developed to cater for the specific accounting needs of businesses working in certain industries.

If you operate in an area with no, or very poor internet connectivity, then a cloud based package may be unsuitable. There aren't too many areas left like this though!

Finally, if you are already using an accounting system – either cloud or desktop based – be very careful before changing to a new system. If your current system meets your needs, is a change necessary? If it is considered necessary, the changeover needs to be planned carefully to:

- Minimise disruption to your accounting activities;
- Avoid data errors or omissions;
- Retain a record of historic transactions (which may be required for many reasons, e.g. to prepare the next set of statutory accounts, or for a tax enquiry); and
- Realise the full benefits of whatever new system you are moving to.

The main cloud providers provide data migration services which can make the whole process *relatively* seamless, but there are various traps for the unwary (which often seem to centre around the VAT account!), so transitions between accounting systems always need to be planned with care. It is often sensible to make the change at the beginning of a new financial year, or if you just can't wait, at the beginning of a new VAT period.

Ultimately, whichever option is chosen – cloud or desktop - the quality of the information you produce from your accounting system will only ever be as good as the quality of the data entered into it. Which takes us to the next chapter.

17

Internal controls for the small business

Some concepts and ideas from the big corporate world translate pretty well into the small business environment, others not so much. One concept that is highly relevant to small businesses, and one which they can definitely benefit from applying, concerns "internal controls".

What do we mean by "internal controls"? Put simply, they are a set of tools and techniques operated by a business that promote effective and efficient operations; reliable financial reporting; and compliance with laws and regulations.

Think of internal controls as a toolkit. Here are the main types of internal control you may use:

- Segregation of duties - dividing up duties between different members of staff in order to reduce the likelihood of fraud or error;

- Organisational controls - establishing clear lines of responsibility and accountability within the organisation;

- Authorisation - having clear authority levels in place, enforced through manual or automated procedures;

- Personnel - having the right people in the right roles, and effectively recruiting, developing and monitoring staff performance;

- Supervision - exercising appropriate day to day supervision and oversight of staff and operations;

- Physical - securing the physical protection and control over access to the company's assets and resources;

- Accounting - using accounting & arithmetical techniques to verify the validity and accuracy of transactions and balances recorded in the financial records; and

- Management - exercising robust management and governance of the organisation in pursuit of the company's overall objectives.

Consider how and where each of the above internal controls may be relevant to the financial processes described in earlier chapters. Internal controls should be built into each process to help secure your intended outcomes.

For example, let's consider the purchases process for a moment. Depending on the scale of your business, one might expect to see:

- Segregation of duties – dividing up the roles of ordering goods, paying the supplier invoices, and recording the transactions in the nominal ledger, in order to reduce the likelihood of errors or fraud (by having more than one person involved, any mistakes are more likely to be identified, and the scope to misappropriate funds by creating a fictitious supplier is much reduced);

- Organisational controls – identifying employees with specific responsibility for different aspects of the purchases process, making it clear who does what;

- Authorisation – establishing limits to what individuals are permitted to do, usually expressed in monetary terms; for example what is the maximum order or maximum supplier payment an individual can make without referral back to the business owner or board;

- Personnel – making sure that personnel involved in the purchases process are of good character and sufficiently trained and able to perform their roles effectively;

- Supervision – overseeing aspects of the purchases process to ensure the different steps in the process are operating as intended;

- Physical – protecting the incoming goods from loss due to theft or other hazards;
- Accounting – checking that purchase transactions and supplier payments have been entered correctly into the accounting system, for example by checking the purchases control account and reviewing the aged creditors report periodically.

Designing internal controls

When deciding what internal controls your business may require, the sequence of thinking goes like this:

1. What are the processes that go on in your business (sales, purchases, stock management etc)?
2. Thinking about each process, what are the things that could go wrong (what are the "risks")?
3. What would be the impact on the business (financial or otherwise) of each risk?
4. Can the likelihood and/ or impact of the risk be reduced cost-effectively to an acceptable level using internal controls?
5. If not, what alternative strategies can be applied to manage the risk?

Controls (such as those described above) can also be classified as either preventive (designed to stop something bad happening) or detective (designed to identify anything bad that has happened).

Preventive control techniques are often more desirable as they are supposed to stop something bad happening in the first place, whereas detective controls serve only to warn management about events that have already occurred.

However all control activities cost money, so the cost of control must also be borne in mind when weighing up what internal controls you will apply.

Limitations

It is important to appreciate that there are limitations to any internal control system; because humans can and do fail, management can override controls, people can collude to circumvent systems, and external events can blow things off course, we can only really concern ourselves with *practical* control, rather than dealing in absolutes.

With this short introduction to internal controls, we have now concluded our review of basic financial processes for the small business. It's now time to move onto part 2 – understanding accounts.

PART 2

UNDERSTANDING ACCOUNTS

18

Why understanding your accounts is vital

Remember, to manage your business finances effectively, you need three things:

- Basic financial procedures to safeguard your business's assets, comply with the law, and produce the financial information you need to be able to manage and grow your business;

- Procedures to monitor and interpret financial information; and

- The ability to tell if everything is "on track", so that if it is not you are in a position to do something about it.

With sound basic financial processes in place, your business's nominal ledger should contain the data you need to be able to produce meaningful financial information. In this part of the book, we are going to look at how you can start to monitor and interpret that information to help you make better decisions.

We're going to identify the main financial reports, and consider how they are used. We will look at some financial words that accountants use and try to demystify them; we'll examine some important financial concepts; and we will also discuss how to interpret what the financial reports mean – what can they tell us about your business's financial performance and position?

Even if you employ a bookkeeper, an accountant, or a whole army of accountants, as the business owner you still absolutely need to know and understand this stuff, because you need to know what is going on, you need to be able to challenge your team and hold them to account; and you need to know what on earth your accountant is talking about!

19

Introducing: the primary financial statements

Have you ever been presented with your business's accounts, only to find you cannot make head nor tail of what they actually mean? If so, you are definitely not alone.

If you don't understand accounts but you have a team who can help you interpret them, then that's great – but this part of the book will still be useful, because without a basic understanding of the accounts, how do you know what questions to ask your team?

Over the following pages we'll take a look at the key things you need to know, covering:

- The balance sheet – this tells you what the business owned or controlled, and what it owed, on a specific date;

- The profit & loss account – this tells you how the business did, financially, in a given period – income, expenses, gains and losses; and

- The cash flow statement – this tells you how much cash the business generated, and what it spent that cash on.

Together, these are known as the "primary financial statements", and you will need to understand what they mean so that you can manage your business finances effectively, ask the right questions, and take the right actions.

A little later on, once we've covered the basics, we'll go into a bit more detail about how to *interpret* what the figures are telling you. Don't worry, though – it's not rocket science. It requires nothing more than a very basic grasp of maths, and a keen interest to better manage and control your business's finances. That's why you're reading this book, right?

20

The value of accounts

What's the point of preparing and reading financial statements? It may seem pretty obvious – yet I'm willing to bet that many small business owners don't spend much time at all looking at "the financials". Many seem to manage with little more than monitoring the bank balance and maybe reviewing amounts owed by customers. Is that sufficient?

I'm guessing, as you are reading this book, that you think maybe there is value in a slightly more disciplined and in-depth approach to financial management. And I would agree! Being able to prepare, read and understand financial reports is incredibly valuable because it helps you:

- Understand the financial implications of the actions you take/ do not take;

- Assess whether your business is generating enough profit to pay yourself and your staff;
- Figure out whether there is enough money to invest in maintaining/ improving the business;
- Identify potential funding shortfalls that you'll need to plug by borrowing and/ or raising share capital;
- Spot opportunities to make more money by adjusting prices or reducing costs; and
- Determine which parts of your business are most successful and whether there are areas of the business that require more attention.

A small investment of time learning how to read and interpret the financial statements should pay dividends in some or all the above areas. The benefits are pretty obvious. By understanding the financials, you'll be better able to identify the key opportunities and problems, ask more relevant questions of your colleagues and advisers, and take more decisive action, leading to better results for your business and greater personal satisfaction for yourself.

21

Management accounts vs statutory accounts

When it comes to accounts there's a lot of terminology that gets used. Don't get too bogged down in all that and do ask your adviser if there's anything you're not sure about! There is, however, one important thing to clarify at this point; the difference between "management accounts" and "statutory accounts".

Statutory accounts (sometimes called "financial accounts", "annual accounts" or "year-end accounts") are the financial statements prepared once a year up to the business's financial year end date. They are backward looking, may be prepared some time after the end of the period, and serve a number of purposes; providing data for management, shareholders and other parties; supplying information for inclusion in corporate or income tax returns; and, in the case of a company, enabling compliance with the requirement to file at Companies House.

Management accounts are also mostly backward looking, but tend to be prepared more frequently, may cover a much shorter period of time than the statutory accounts, and their primary purpose is to help management control the business and make decisions that have a financial aspect.

Management accounts are often presented in a slightly different way to the annual statutory accounts, but the overriding principles apply equally to either type of accounts so for the purposes of this book generally we refer to both types.

22

Whose job is it to prepare the accounts?

Whose job is it to prepare accounts? As the business owner, that's up to you. But someone, somewhere, does need to be doing it. Running a business with no financial information is a bit like driving a car with your eyes shut. Neither is very sensible and both, inevitably, lead to disaster!

If your business trades as a limited company, the form and content of your year-end, statutory accounts is dictated by the Companies Act 2006 and UK accounting guidance, and it is highly likely you will use a professional accountant to prepare them. If your business is structured as a sole trade or partnership, there are fewer rules about how the year-end accounts should be prepared, but you'll probably still use an accountant to prepare them. And that's all good because preparing year-end accounts can be a complex business and it needs to be done right.

Where the management accounts are concerned – those accounts you should be using regularly to help manage your business – a variety of approaches are adopted by small businesses. Depending on the scale of your business, its stage of development, and the skills of the people on your team, you may prepare management accounts yourself, with the help of your staff, or you may outsource this to your accountant. Or indeed a combination. There's no right or wrong answer here - as long as someone is doing it and doing it properly!

Preparing good quality financial statements does depend on having reliable underlying transaction data so you'll need suitable processes and controls in place to capture and record all the details of your business's income and expenses, in an accurate and timely way, as discussed in part 1 of this book.

Whereas the statutory accounts would normally be prepared once per annum, management accounts should be produced more frequently, as this aids more timely decision making. Again there's no 'one size fits all' answer, but for many small businesses a system of producing management accounts on a monthly or quarterly basis seems to work well.

23

Basic accounting concepts

Before we go any further, we need to get clear on a few basic accounting concepts. I appreciate this may seem a bit dry, but the truth is, if you want to get a really solid grip on your business finances (and why wouldn't you?), you have to understand this stuff. This is the foundation of much that I discuss elsewhere in this book. So let's talk about:

- Assets;
- Liabilities;
- Equity;
- Balance sheets;
- The fundamental rule;

- Capital employed;
- Liquidity; and
- Solvency.

Assets

An asset, simply, is a resource that a business owns or controls. Examples might include premises owned by the business; stocks of materials or goods held for resale; money owed to the business by customers; and money held at the bank or in cash. Parties who owe money to the business are often referred to as "debtors".

Liabilities

A liability, basically, is an obligation of a business to pay another party, in cash or in kind. Examples might include amounts due to suppliers; taxes due to HMRC; amounts due to the bank under overdrafts or term loans; wages payable to employees; and dividends payable to investors. The terms "liabilities" and "creditors" are often used interchangeably.

Equity

The business owners' financial interest in a business. In a company, this is the share capital plus all the profits that have not been paid out to shareholders.

Balance sheets

A balance sheet, essentially, is a table that shows a business's assets and liabilities, on a specific date.

The fundamental rule

The assets of a business are always equal to the sum of its liabilities and its owners' interest in the business. Assets = liabilities + equity. This is the fundamental rule of accounts, as illustrated below:

DEBITS	CREDITS
Assets	Liabilities
	Equity

Capital employed

The assets of a business, less its short-term liabilities. Capital employed is the value of the assets a business uses to generate income.

Liquidity

Liquidity refers to a business's ability to pay (settle) its short term liabilities as they fall due. Some assets are said to be "more liquid" than others – that means that they are more readily turned into cash.

Solvency

Solvency refers to a business's ability to pay whatever it owes to third parties - including longer term borrowing. A business is said to be technically insolvent when its total liabilities exceed its total assets.

24

The balance sheet

The balance sheet is a financial snapshot of your business on a specific day.

In simple terms, it shows a value for items that the business owns or controls (known as "assets"); a value for items that the business owes ("liabilities"); and it also explains how the business is funded ("equity" or "reserves").

A balance sheet tells us lots of useful things about the financial health of a business and answers lots of important questions; does it have sufficient resources to meet its financial obligations?; how is it funded?; how resilient is the business to unforeseen economic shocks?; can the business sustain additional borrowing?

Small business financial management

To illustrate the concept, we can imagine for a moment that an individual is quite like a business in some ways. An individual can own assets and bear liabilities just like a business can. So let's draw up a balance sheet for an individual, we'll call her Mrs Smith.

Mrs Smith

Balance sheet

As at 30 April 2019

	£
ASSETS	
House	250,000
Car	5,000
Investments	10,000
Personal effects	8,000
Bank balance	1,000
TOTAL ASSETS	**274,000**
LIABILITIES	
Mortgage on house	(200,000)
Credit card balance	(1,500)
Loan from friend	(500)
TOTAL LIABILITIES	**(202,000)**
NET WORTH (274,000 - £202,000)	**72,000**

The balance sheet

Why are the liabilities shown in brackets? This simply means they are "minus" numbers. It's just how accountants show "minus" numbers - that's all.

So, Mrs Smith has assets adding up to £274,000 and liabilities adding up to £202,000, and the difference between the two, £72,000, is what she is said to be worth (purely in a financial sense, of course!).

Mrs Smith's net worth on 30th April 2019 is the total of all she has ever been given and all she has ever earned, less anything she has ever given away or lost, and everything she owes to someone else on that date.

If you wish, you can draw up your own personal balance sheet now. See how you compare to Mrs Smith!

Small business financial management

Let's now look at a balance sheet for a business. You'll see that it's really not so different from Mrs Smith's personal balance sheet:

ABC Company Ltd

Balance sheet

As at 30 April 2019

	£	£
FIXED ASSETS		
Property		550,000
CURRENT ASSETS		
Stock	10,000	
Trade debtors	230,000	
Bank	-	
	240,000	
CREDITORS FALLING DUE WITHIN ONE YEAR		
Trade creditors	(120,000)	
Bank overdraft	(15,000)	
Taxes due to HMRC	(45,000)	
	(180,000)	
NET CURRENT ASSETS		**60,000**
TOTAL ASSETS LESS CURRENT LIABILITIES		**610,000**

CREDITORS FALLING DUE AFTER MORE THAN ONE YEAR

Bank loan	(300,000)
NET ASSETS	**310,000**

CAPITAL AND RESERVES

Share capital	1,000
Profit and loss account	309,000
SHAREHOLDERS' FUNDS	**310,000**

We've got some new words introduced here, but keep in mind that all we are really doing is showing the company's assets and liabilities – what it owns and controls, less what it owes – and its shareholders funds (which is just the number you get when you start with the assets then take away the liabilities). It's basically the exact same idea as with Mrs Smith's balance sheet.

Let's explore what some of those new words mean (there's also a handy glossary at the end of the book as well that you can refer to whenever you want!).

An asset is a resource controlled by the business as a result of past events and from which future economic benefits are expected to be realised, usually in the form of cash or cash equivalents.

Most assets have a physical form, but some do not. The right of ownership is not essential; for example, property held on a lease may still be an asset, if the business controls the benefits that are expected to flow from the property. Here are some examples of assets:

- Land & buildings;
- Plant & equipment;
- Software;
- Leases;
- Goodwill;
- Investments;
- Stock;
- Amounts owed by customers ("trade debtors");
- Bank & cash balances;
- Loans to the directors.

Assets are further subdivided into "fixed" or "non-current" assets – those held for the long term, like property or equipment; and "current assets" – typically more liquid assets with a shorter lifecycle, like money in a current account or amounts owed by customers.

Fixed assets

Fixed assets are things the business owns or controls that are held for ongoing use in the business.

They can be tangible (things you can see and touch, like a building, plant & machinery, office equipment and vehicles); intangible (things you can't see or touch, like computer software or a patent); and investments (like money invested in another company).

ABC's fixed assets consist of a property with a "book value" (the value shown in the accounts) of £550,000. This is not necessarily its current value – in fact it probably isn't. We'll come back to this point later on.

Current assets

Current assets are things the business owns or controls, that are not fixed assets. In other words they are "used up" or "consumed" or "turned over" more quickly than fixed assets.

The most common examples are stocks of goods held for resale/ raw materials for production; amounts owed by customers ("trade debtors"); and money held in the bank/ in cash. ABC's current assets have a total book value of £240,000, made up of some stock, and money due from customers.

Current assets are said to be more "liquid" than fixed assets – remember, that means they can often be turned into cash more quickly than fixed assets. We'll come back to liquidity later on.

Assets are normally shown in the balance sheet at either "depreciated historic cost" – basically their original cost of acquisition, less, in some cases, depreciation; or "fair value" – basically an estimate of their current market value at the balance sheet date.

A liability is a present obligation arising from past events, the settlement of which will result in an outflow of resources. The obligation may be a legally enforceable obligation, such as an amount payable to someone under a contract; or a constructive obligation, which may arise where third parties have an expectation of settlement arising from past practice, published policies or some other undertaking that has been given by the business.

Here are some examples of liabilities (what your business owes):

- Amounts owed to suppliers ("trade creditors");
- Bank overdrafts and loans;
- Amounts due under hire purchase/ finance lease arrangements;
- Business tax liabilities.

Liabilities are further subdivided between short and longer term amounts; those amounts due within, and after more than, one year from the date to which the accounts are made up.

Liabilities are normally shown in the balance sheet date at "amortised cost" – basically the amount payable. Longer term liabilities may be discounted, reflecting that a debt of £100 payable in ten or twenty years will probably be much less of an economic burden than a debt of £100 payable next week.

Current liabilities

When a business enters into some kind of contract or agreement with another party that will involve it paying that party – in cash or in kind – at some future point, that is a liability.

Mrs Smith took out a mortgage on her house; spent money on her credit card; and borrowed money from a friend; all these things are liabilities.

In a business context, liabilities can arise for all sorts of reasons; common examples including buying things from suppliers on credit ("trade creditors"); using a bank overdraft or borrowing on a long term bank loan; and owing money to the taxman.

Current liabilities are liabilities that a business expects to have to "settle" (i.e. pay) within a year of the date that the balance sheet is drawn up to. ABC's current liabilities total £180,000.

Net current assets

The difference between a business's current assets and its current liabilities is known as "net current assets".

In ABC's case, that's £60,000. It is a really interesting number – honestly! Remember that *current* assets are those assets that a business uses, consumes or turns over quite quickly; and *current* liabilities are those liabilities that a business has to pay within a short space of time. Working out net current assets can tell us something important about a business's ability to settle its short term liabilities on time – to pay its suppliers, pay the taxman, pay the bank loan etc.

This is what we mean when we talk about "liquidity", and it's quite possible for a business to have net current *liabilities* – where the current liabilities total more than the current assets. A business with net current liabilities *could* have a big problem paying its bills on time, because it *may* not have enough cash - and other assets that can be readily turned into cash (such as stock or amounts due from customers) - to be able to pay its suppliers, staff, or the taxman on time.

If you're already in business, take a look now at the last balance sheet your accountant prepared for you. Is it telling you anything interesting about your business's net current assets (or net current liabilities)?

Creditors falling due after more than one year

Liabilities that are not due to be settled (paid) within a year of the balance sheet date go in this category, which is sometimes called simply "long term liabilities".

The most common examples are long term bank loans and asset finance arrangements (e.g. hire purchase). Longer term liabilities that are repayable in regular instalments (like most bank loans and asset finance contracts) are split between the two categories of liability; those instalments falling due within a year of the balance sheet date are included in current liabilities; those falling due after more than a year go into this category. ABC has a bank loan with instalments falling due after more than one year totalling £300,000.

Net assets

Net assets is simply the difference between all the business's asset and all its liabilities. ABC has net assets of £310,000. It is possible for a business to have net liabilities – where its total liabilities exceeds its total assets. Such a business is said to be "technically insolvent". This does not *necessarily* mean that the business will fail, or even that it is in difficulty, but a balance sheet with net liabilities would normally provoke further investigation.

Capital and reserves – "equity" or "capital employed"

If your business is a company, its balance sheet will show "capital and reserves". The capital and reserves section tells us how the investors have funded the company. Other names for this are "equity" and "capital employed" and it is basically made up of two things: share capital; and accumulated profits to date, less amounts paid out to investors to date as dividends – otherwise known as "retained earnings" or "retained profits".

What is share capital? What do we mean by "retained profits"?

Share capital

Share capital is money invested into a company by investors in return for a share of ownership, the right to have a say in how the company is run, the right to share in the profits of the company (through "dividends"), and the right to receive a share of the proceeds if the company is sold or closed down ("wound up").

The money paid to the company as share capital becomes the company's money – ordinary share capital is not repayable to the investors at some future point, so it is not a liability.

ABC has £1,000 of share capital. Often, especially in smaller companies, the share capital may be quite a small number - £100 or even £1!

Profit & loss account – "retained earnings"

The other part of the capital and reserves section is the profit & loss account, sometimes known as "retained profits", "retained reserves", or "distributable profits". This figure is made up of all the company's historic profits, less all the company's historic losses, less all dividends previously paid to shareholders.

ABC has £309,000 of retained earnings.

Dividends are paid to a company's shareholders out of the profits a company makes; whatever profits are not paid out to shareholders are "retained" i.e. kept in the company. These retained profits help fund the company's ongoing activities. We'll look at dividends a bit more later on in the book.

The fundamental rule of accounts – in practice

Here, finally, we get to the magic part: how it all fits together. Why we call a balance sheet a balance sheet. What it all means! Well done if you're still with me...

Go back to ABC's balance sheet for a moment – do you notice anything interesting? Take a look at the values for NET ASSETS and SHAREHOLDERS' FUNDS – did you notice they are the same number, £310,000? That's no coincidence! They are the same number – they "balance".

Unless your accountant is having a *really* bad day, any balance sheet they produce for you will always show these two numbers in balance. Why is this? Remember the fundamental rule of accounts:

ASSETS = LIABILITIES + EQUITY

Or put another way

ASSETS – LIABILITIES = EQUITY

As far as *any* balance sheet is concerned, the assets of a business – all the property, equipment, money in the bank, stock amounts owed by customers – must *always* be equal to the liabilities of the business – all the amounts owed to suppliers, the taxman, the bank – plus the investors' stake in the business. There are *no* exceptions.

The reason? Because any asset on the balance sheet must ultimately have been funded by one (or more) of the following sources:

1. Capital provided by investors (that's equity);
2. Accumulated profits (that's also equity);
3. By incurring a liability (that's a liability); or
4. By exchanging one asset for another (e.g. paying for stock with cash, or receiving cash from a customer for sales that were made on credit).

Going back to ABC one more time:

ASSETS = LIABILITIES + EQUITY

- Assets total £550,000 + £240,000 = £790,000

- Liabilities total £180,000 + £300,000 = £480,000
- Equity totals £310,000
- £790,000 = £480,000 + £310,000

And

NET ASSETS = EQUITY

- Net assets = £790,000 - £480,000 = £310,000

And we can also illustrate ABC's balance sheet this way:

DEBITS	CREDITS
Assets £790,000	Liabilities £480,000
	Equity £310,000

Businesses that are sole trades or partnerships

Businesses that are run as sole trades or partnerships will not have share capital because there are no shareholders, only an individual or group of individuals who work together in partnership. So the balance sheet for a sole trade or partnership does not have a capital and reserves section, instead it shows the financial interest the individual (or each individual partner) has in the business.

This is basically the amount of money (and other assets) they have put in, plus their share of accumulated profits, less their share of accumulated losses, less amounts they have taken out ("drawings").

For most practical purposes, though, the concepts are broadly the same as described for companies. You can interchange "capital and reserves" with "partners' capital/ current accounts".

25

The profit & loss account

The profit & loss account is your business's financial scorecard, explaining what income it earned in a specific period, and what expenses it incurred. The balance sheet tells us what shape the runner is in at the end of the marathon; the profit & loss account tells us how well she ran the race, so to speak.

Defining income and expenses

Everyone's got a pretty good idea what the term "income" means, but here's the technical definition: income is defined as an increase in economic benefits in the form of inflows or enhancements of assets or decreases of liabilities that result in increases in equity, other than those arising from equity contributions from investors. Inflows of money or other resources to a business from investors are not income!

Income includes both revenue – that is, income arising in the course of ordinary activities undertaken by the business – and also gains, which are also income but not revenue. Gains happen when a business sells a fixed asset for more than it is valued at in the accounts. Gains may be reported separately on a statement of comprehensive income.

Everyone's also got a pretty good idea what the term "expenses" means, too. Here's the technical definition: expenses are defined as decreases in economic benefits in the form of outflows or depletions of assets or incurrences of liabilities that result in decreases in equity, other than those relating to distributions to investors. Outflows of money or other resources from a business to investors are not expenses!

Expenses include those arising in the course of ordinary activities undertaken by the business, and also losses, such as losses arising on the disposal of fixed assets.

Why a profit & loss account is useful

The profit & loss account is helpful because it tells us whether the business is profitable; a business that is not profitable, in the long run is not sustainable. And if you can figure out how profitable your business is, you can make important decisions about things like how much to pay everybody; how much you can reinvest into the business; and whether you need to raise additional money to grow the business.

The difference between profits and cash flows

The profit & loss account is not a report of cash in and out. That's why it's described in terms of "income earned" and "expenses incurred", rather than "money received" and "money paid". What the profit & loss account does is measure the amount of *value generated*, and of course there are things of value beyond money held in the bank.

For example, if my business sells you £100 of goods on credit, your debt to my business still has value, even though it hasn't yet been paid. The money might not yet be in my business's bank account, but that doesn't mean it hasn't earned anything. It's earned £100 – assuming it does eventually get paid, of course!

So the profit & loss account is all about measuring the financial value of the transactions that a business enters into within a specific timeframe – not flows of cash in or out. In accounting parlance this idea is known as the "accruals concept".

Still confused? Don't worry, you're not alone. I'll offer some specific examples which will hopefully make thing a little clearer.

Let's take a look at a simple profit & loss account. Here we have "EZCo Ltd", an ordinary company limited by shares. What are we looking at here?

EZCo Ltd

Profit & loss account

For the year ended 30 April 2019

	2019	2018
	£	£
TURNOVER	150,000	60,000
Cost of sales	(80,000)	(30,000)
GROSS PROFIT	**70,000**	**30,000**
Selling and distribution costs	(5,000)	(4,000)
Administrative expenses	(30,000)	(32,000)
Other operating income	-	1,000
OPERATING PROFIT/ (LOSS)	**35,000**	**(5,000)**
Interest receivable and similar income	2,000	2,000
Interest payable and similar charges	(8,000)	-
PROFIT/ (LOSS) BEFORE TAXATION	**29,000**	**(3,000)**
Tax on profit/ (loss)	(5,000)	1,000
PROFIT/ (LOSS) FOR THE FINANCIAL YEAR	**24,000**	**(2,000)**

Let's work our way through, starting at the top. The first thing to notice is right at the top – we have the business's name; and it says the period that the profit & loss account covers; remember, a profit & loss account reports on the income & expenses for a specific period. In this case it's a year, but the period could be longer or shorter – it doesn't necessarily matter, but the period should always be stated.

The second thing to notice is the general layout of the profit & loss account. Down the left, we have different descriptions, which tell us what the numbers on the right relate to. On the right hand side, we have two columns of numbers, and you'll see that each of the two columns is headed up with a different year.

The column of numbers on the left is the numbers for the period stated at the top: the year ended 30th April 2019. The column of numbers on the right, is the figures that were reported for the previous period, i.e. the period ended 30th April 2018. These numbers are called the "comparative numbers" or "comparatives" for short, and they are usually shown so the reader can compare the latest financial figures with those of the previous period. The balance sheet and cash flow statement also normally show the comparative numbers for the preceding period – to keep things simple we didn't shown them in the example of ABC in the preceding chapter.

OK, I hope you're still with me! Next, let's work our way down the numbers, starting with "Turnover".

Turnover

Turnover is the business's income *earned* in the period, before deducting any costs. If your business is VAT registered, it will normally exclude the VAT (as your business basically just collects the VAT from customers and pays it over to HMRC, VAT is not part of your business's income).

EZCo's turnover for the year ended 30th April 2019 was £150,000; for the year ended 30th April 2018 it was £60,000. This means that EZCo *earned* income of £150,000 in the latest period – it does not necessarily mean that it *invoiced* £150,000, and it does not mean that it *received* £150,000. But it earned £150,000 – that's the amount of money, excluding VAT, that EZCo became entitled to receive from its customers as a result of all work done in the period. Simple!

Cost of sales

Next up, "Cost of sales". Costs of sale are normally the day to day business costs most closely associated with generating the products or services your business sells. Contrast this with "Administrative expenses", shown further down the profit & loss account, which tend to be seen more as an "overhead".

Costs of sale are likely to vary in relation to the volume/ value of sales achieved in any period; administrative expenses tend to be rather more "fixed" from one period to the next and have less of a direct relationship to the amount of sales achieved.

EZCo's cost of sales in its most recent financial year was £80,000; in the previous year £30,000. Notice how the total cost of sales has gone up roughly in the same proportion as sales, from £30,000 to £80,000 / from £60,000 to £150,000.

Costs typically included in cost of sales:

- Goods or raw materials bought in for further processing/resale;
- Productive labour costs, including subcontract costs;
- Other costs bearing a direct relationship to sales.

Costs typically included in administrative expenses:

- Premises expenses if the premises are used for administrative purposes (light & heat, rates, insurance);
- Office expenses (phone, internet, stationery);
- Marketing & advertising costs.

Note that costs shown in the profit & loss account are the costs *incurred* in the period – not necessarily the amounts *invoiced* by suppliers, or the amounts actually *paid*. If your business is VAT registered, then the costs shown in the profit & loss account will normally exclude VAT (since your business is probably able to recover the VAT from HMRC, VAT is not part of your business's expenses).

Selling and distribution costs

Depending on the business, distribution costs – that is, the costs of distributing your product or service - may be shown as a separate category, or included within costs of sale or administrative expenses. EZCo's selling and distribution costs totalled £5,000 in "2018/19" (its most recent financial year).

Other operating income

Other operating income may include income from sources other than ordinary sales to customers – for example it may include government grants, insurance claims, or gains on foreign exchange transactions.

EZCo had none in the latest financial year, but £1,000 in the previous year. Because there was a number for the comparative year, we show other operating income in its profit & loss account – but if EZCo had no operating income in either the current or comparative year, we would simply take out the "other operating income" line altogether.

Operating profit (or loss)

Operating profit is the sum of all of the above – in other words, the amount of net income generated through the business's trading activities.

EZCo's operating profit was £35,000. In the previous period it was a loss of £5,000 - which is why that number is shown in brackets.

Interest receivable and similar income

Interest receivable and similar income will include income from investments. It's still income, but typically it is generated from passive investment of the business's resources, rather than from active trading activities.

Interest payable and similar charges

Interest payable and similar charges represents the cost of raising and paying for the business's finance, typically this will include interest payable on things like bank loans and overdrafts, and on lease and hire-purchase type arrangements.

EZCo had £8,000 of interest payable and similar charges in 2018/19 but none in the previous year. Perhaps it took out an interest-bearing loan, went into overdraft with the bank, or entered into a hire purchase arrangement sometime in the latest financial year?

Profit (or loss) before taxation

Profit before taxation does what it says on the tin; it's the profit (or loss) that arose in the specified period, before taxation is applied.

EZCo made a pre-tax profit of £29,000; the previous year it made a loss of £3,000.

Tax on profit (or loss)

Taxation is the recognition of tax costs (or credits) associated with the profit (or loss) made in the period. You'll see this in company profit & loss accounts, because companies in the UK are liable to pay corporation tax on their profits.

Sole trade and partnership profit & loss accounts, by contrast, won't show this line because the tax liabilities arising on the profits are payable by the individuals, not by the business.

EZCo's tax charge – its tax expense - totalled £5,000; we know it's an expense because the figure is in brackets. In the comparative period, the figure was a £1,000 credit – in other words, income.

The tax charge (or credit) in the accounts is rarely the amount of money the company will have to pay to (or recover from) HMRC. It is often *approximately* the same, but because there is a different set of rules for working out profits *for tax purposes*, we end up with "timing differences". We'll come back to that later in the book.

Profit (or loss) for the financial year

Profit (or loss) for the financial year does what it says on the tin; it's the amount of profit (or loss) remaining after deducting (or adding back) the tax charges (or credits). EZCo made £24,000 in the latest year, but lost £2,000 "after tax" in the prior period.

Retained profits are also sometimes also shown in the profit & loss account of a company, because companies don't necessarily keep (retain) all of the profits they make; often companies pay the shareholders dividends out of the profits they make. So some profit & loss accounts also show dividends and retained profits.

26

Reporting income and expenditure - important concepts

While we're on the subject of profits and losses, we need to review a couple of important concepts.

Capital vs revenue expenditure

One crucially important point to remember in all of this is that certain expenses do not appear in the profit & loss account at all. The profit & loss account is designed to show income earned and expenses incurred in a specified period, but where a business acquires something of significant and lasting value - for example, a building, or a patent, or some computer software – it is inappropriate to say that the benefit of the expenditure has been entirely consumed in the period of acquisition.

Many assets in fact have an enduring benefit to the business extending many years into the future, generating revenues directly or indirectly over many accounting periods. What I am referring to here is the important distinction between revenue and capital expenditure. The former represents expenditure on items that are, broadly speaking, consumed within a single accounting period. The latter represents expenditure on items that provide a more enduring benefit to the business.

Such items are "capitalised" on the balance sheet and the costs are then gradually transferred to the profit & loss account in stages over the estimated "useful economic life" of the asset in question. That is what a "depreciation" or "amortisation" charge seeks to do – gradually recognise in the profit & loss account the "using up" of an asset over more than one financial period.

Matching income and expenses

We've already discussed the idea that income and expenses are shown in the profit & loss account for the financial period in which they are earned/ incurred – not necessarily the same period that the cash flows into or out of the business. Remember this is known as the "accruals concept".

Another important idea says that a business's expenses should be shown in profit & loss account in the same financial period as the income they helped to generate – this is known as the "matching concept". We want to include the expenses and the related income in the same period, not different periods, so that the profit & loss account fairly represents what happened in the period, neither overstating nor understating the profit (or loss).

Earnings before interest, taxation, depreciation and amortisation (EBITDA)

You may have heard of the phrase "EBITDA" which stands for "earnings before interest, taxation, depreciation and amortisation". EBITDA is a measurement used to gauge a business's ability to generate profits, without taking into account how it is financed (the interest costs), how it is taxed (the taxation costs), or capital costs (the depreciation and amortisation).

It is sometimes used to try to gauge a business's ability to generate cash inflows from its operating activities - though it is no real substitute for a proper cash flow statement (see next chapter!). Lenders and investors sometimes use EBITDA to assess how a company is doing, compare it against competitors or against prior periods.

EBITDA can be worked out from a business's profit & loss account by taking the operating profit and then adding back depreciation and amortisation charges.

27

The cash flow statement

The cash flow statement explains how your business generates cash; and how it spends it. As we have already seen, cash flow is not the same as profit/ loss. It tells us something different, but equally important. Even very profitable businesses can run into problems if cash flow is not managed carefully. So we need a way to report the flows of money into and out of a business – that's what the cash flow statement does. Let's take a look at this example:

Munee Ltd

Cash flow statement

For the year ended 30 April 2019

	2019	2018
	£	£

CASH FLOWS FROM OPERATING ACTIVITIES

Cash generated from operations	50,000	45,000
Taxation paid	(12,000)	(5,000)
NET CASH GENERATED FROM OPERATIONS	**38,000**	**40,000**
CASH FLOWS FROM INVESTING ACTIVITIES		
Proceeds from sale of tangible assets	3,000	-
Purchase of property, plant & equipment	-	(8,000)
Purchase of intangible assets	-	(2,000)
Interest received	1,000	1,000
NET CASH USED IN INVESTING ACTUIVITIES	**4,000**	**(9,000)**
CASH FLOWS FROM FINANCING ACTIVITIES		
Issue of ordinary share capital	-	1,000
Repayment of bank loans	(10,000)	(10,000)
Repayment of finance lease obligations	(1,000)	-
Interest paid	(1,000)	(1,000)
Dividends paid	(2,000)	-
NET CASH USED IN FINANCING ACTIVITIES	**(14,000)**	**(10,000)**
NET INCREASE/ (DECREASE) IN CASH AND CASH EQUIVALENTS	28,000	21,000
Cash and cash equivalents at beginning of year	26,000	5,000
CASH AND CASH EQUIVALENTS AT END OF YEAR	**54,000**	**26,000**

A cash flow statement normally breaks down a business's cash flow into three sections:

Cash flow from operating activities

This represents money received and paid in respect of the business's normal trading activities; for example money received from customers for the goods and services they buy, money paid to suppliers for goods and services received, and wages paid to employees.

Munee generated £50,000 of cash inflows from its operations in the year ended 30th April 2019, and paid to HMRC £12,000 of corporation tax on its trading profits, so it had net cash inflows from operating activities of £38,000. In the prior period its net cash inflow from operations was a little higher, £40,000.

Cash flow from investing activities

This represents cash flows associated with investments made in the business; for example money paid to acquire fixed assets, money received on the disposal of fixed assets, and money paid to buy shares in other companies.

In our example, Munee had net cash inflows from investing activities of £4,000 in the latest reporting period; but net cash *out*flows of £9,000 in 2017/18. We know it's a net outflow because it's in brackets, so it's a minus number.

Cash flow from financing activities

This represents cash flows associated with how the business is financed; for example receipts of capital from issuing shares; money repaid to lenders; dividends paid to shareholders.

Munee had net cash outflows from financing activities of £14,000 in 2018/19 and net cash outflows of £10,000 in the previous year.

Cash and cash equivalents at beginning/ end of year

Notice how the last three rows of the cash flow statement explain how the business's cash balances (and "cash equivalents", which basically means investments that can be readily turned into cash) change over the course of the period.

The balance at the end of the comparative period, in our example £26,000, is the same as the balance at the start of the current period. The overall cash inflow (or outflow) is added to (or deducted from) the starting cash balance, to arrive at the cash balance at the end of the period, in Munee's case £54,000. The cash balance at the end of the period should match the balance stated in the balance sheet.

28

Preparing and interpreting the cash flow statement

The cash flow statement tells us some important things about the business's ability to generate money; reinvest in essential areas; and meet its obligations to creditors and shareholders. The profit & loss account and balance sheet on their own don't tell the full story.

Having net cash *out*flows from investing or financing activities is not necessarily a bad thing; businesses have to reinvest money to keep everything working and they often borrow money to help them grow. What does really matter is that the cash inflows from operating activities should exceed the total of any outflows from investing and financing activities, at least most of the time! If the business has enough cash, it may be able to weather total decreases in cash in the short term; but probably not in the long run.

Preparation

There are two main methods to prepare the cash flow statement; the indirect and direct methods.

Under the indirect method, cash flow from operating activities is determined by starting with profits as reported in the profit & loss account and then adjusting that figure for changes over the period in stock, trade debtors and trade creditors; and removing non-cash items such as depreciation.

Under the direct method, net cash flow from operating activities is presented by disclosing information about major classes of gross cash receipts and payments, which may be obtained either from the accounting records of the business, or by taking the details of sales, costs of sale and other items from the profit & loss account and then adjusting them in a similar manner to that described for the indirect method.

Many small companies – and nearly all sole traders and partnerships – will not prepare a cash flow statement as part of their year end accounts, as it is generally required only for larger companies and companies whose accounts are audited. But it may be a good idea to prepare one from time to time anyway, since a cash flow statement will tell you things about your cash flows that will not be evident from the profit & loss account and balance sheet.

29

Notes to the accounts

The year-end statutory accounts usually contain additional information about a business's financial performance and position in the form of "notes" or "disclosures". The notes, which appear at the back of the accounts, often go into greater detail about some of the amounts shown in the profit & loss account, balance sheet or cash flow statement.

In addition, they explain the business's accounting policies (the approach it takes to prepare its accounts and the UK accounting standards applied), and may provide information about some matters not otherwise shown on the face of the three primary statements, including:

- Breakdowns of all the significant balances in the balance sheet;

- Numbers of employees;
- Amounts loaned by a company to its directors;
- Securities granted by a company to third parties; and
- Commitments under leases (that will result in future cash outflows).

Reading the notes is *always* worthwhile if you want to try to understand what your accounts (or your competitors!) are *really* telling you.

30

Qualitative aspects of financial statements

The following qualitative aspects of financial statements are listed in the UK Financial Reporting Standard FRS 102. They're a pretty good guide to the characteristics of good quality financial statements that are prepared to aid economic decision-making and report on the financial stewardship of management. If this all sounds a bit too esoteric for your tastes, just skip this chapter!

Understandability

Information in the financial statements should be understandable – that is, comprehensible to a user who has a reasonable knowledge of business and economic and accounting activities.

Relevance

The information provided must be relevant to the decision-making needs of users, enabling them to evaluate past, present or future events or confirm or correct their past evaluations.

Materiality

Information is considered material if its omission or misstatement, individually or collectively, could influence the economic decisions that users take on the basis of the financial statements. Financial statements should be free from material misstatements – but this does not necessarily mean that financial statements are completely error-free!

Reliability

Information presented in financial statements should be free from material error and bias, representing faithfully what actually happened.

Substance over form

Transactions and other events should be accounted for and presented in accordance with their underlying substance, not merely their legal form. This enhances the reliability of financial statements.

Prudence

The uncertainties that surround many events and circumstances should be acknowledged in the financial statements by exercising prudence – that is, applying a degree of caution when preparing financial statements to ensure that assets and income are not overstated and liabilities and expenses are not understated (but without introducing bias).

Completeness

Information in the financial statements should be complete, within the bounds of materiality and cost, as omissions can cause information to be false or misleading and thus unreliable.

Comparability

The measurement and display of transactions and events should be undertaken in a consistent manner from one period to the next an across different entities, so that users can identify trends and evaluate relative financial performance and position. Accounting policies should also be disclosed along with details of any changes thereto.

Timeliness

To be relevant, financial statements need to be prepared on a timely basis, within the decision-making timeframe of the users.

Balance between benefit and cost

The benefits derived from information should exceed the cost of producing it.

It's now time to move on to part 3 where we explore in depth how to manage your small business's finances, using your accounts and other financial information...

PART 3

MANAGING THE FINANCES

31

Knowledge is power

What do we mean by "managing the finances"?

To recap, if you want to control your business finances effectively, you need to have all of the following in place:

- Basic financial procedures to safeguard your business's assets, comply with the law, and produce the financial information you need to be able to manage and grow your business;

- Procedures to monitor and interpret financial information; and

- The ability to tell if everything is "on track", so that if it is not you are in a position to do something about

In this part of the book we move on to how you, as the business owner, can actively anticipate – or identify – financial issues and opportunities so that you are in a good position to keep things on track.

Here we are concerned with the big picture – not the nitty gritty, day to day stuff, but dealing with the bigger managerial and strategic financial issues. You need to be able to see the wood, not just the trees!

By equipping you with a little knowledge about financial management techniques, I am hoping that you'll be able to exercise greater control over your business's finances and make better financial decisions.

32

Managing cash flows

Cash flows and profits are not the same thing. I keep saying it – and it's true! When managing your business finances, you need to manage *both*.

Very profitable businesses – especially those that are growing fast – can fail because they did not have sufficient cash coming in to be able to pay the bills. So, you need to monitor and plan your cash flows, not just your profits. That's where cash flow forecasting enters the picture.

You may wish to prepare cash flow forecasts regularly, for relatively shorter periods of time – perhaps monthly or quarterly, depending on the business and how "tight" cash is.

Small business financial management

The point is to identify any potential cash shortfalls *before* they happen, so you have time to put some corrective actions in place. Going to the bank when the business is already at (or beyond) its overdraft limit and it can't pay its staff or suppliers is never a good look.

Here's an example of a cash flow template, based on a spreadsheet approach, for a six week period:

	Wk 1	Wk 2	Wk 3	Wk 4	Wk 5	Wk 6	Total
RECEIPTS							
Sales invoiced							
from debtors							
Capital introduced							
TOTAL INFLOWS							
PAYMENTS							
Purchases for resale							
Salaries							
Other costs of sale							
Motor/ travel							
Insurance							
Repairs & maint							
Rent & rates							
Heat & light							

Other office expenses						
Bank interest						
Capital expenses						
Dividends						
VAT/ other taxes						
Loans						
Dividends						
TOTAL OUTFLOWS						
NET CASH FLOW						
Cash balance b/f						
CASH BALANCE C/F						

Tips for preparing a cash flow forecast

- Remember that we are concerned with actual *cash* inflows and outflows so, unlike with a profit & loss account, we want to show income and expenditure flows *including the VAT*, where applicable;

- Include capital expenditure (money spent on fixed assets);

- Payments to business owners (as dividends or drawings) and to lenders need to be included;
- Tax cash flows need to be included too (including monthly/ quarterly VAT payments/ recoveries; PAYE payments; and corporation tax payments/ repayments).

If your forecast reveals that your business will have insufficient cash resources (taking into account any available overdraft facility), you will need to take urgent action to remedy the situation. Read the chapter "Cash flow crisis management" for some suggestions.

Tips for improving cash flow

- Agree terms before taking on work;
- Lease or hire rather than buying;
- Monitor working capital the whole time – know how much working capital would be needed if sales grew by 10 or 20% and make sure you have enough working capital available (we'll get back to working capital shortly);
- Invoice customers as soon as you can;
- Incentivise customers to pay early;
- Restrict the amount of credit offered to customers;
- Monitor late payers and escalate chasing activity promptly;
- Don't overstock;

- Sell off obsolete/ underused assets;
- Make sure you are taking advantage of all tax reliefs and exemptions;
- Increase your prices, reduce your costs, and sell more;
- Cut back discretionary/ unproductive spend.

Cash flow forecasting software can make the job of forecasting slightly easier; there is a number of programs available, some of which can integrate with accounting software, for example Futrli and Float.

33

Budgeting & forecasting

In this chapter we'll focus on creating a budgeted profit & loss account and balance sheet.

Cash flows were considered in the previous chapter – however there's no practical reason why you can't prepare a budgeted profit & loss account, balance sheet, and a cash flow forecast all at the same time, and many businesses do. I've just separated out the topics here for clarity.

Anyway, why have a budget? And what's the difference between a budget and a forecast?

A budget is basically a financial representation of what the owners expect to achieve over a set period of time. A budget is useful for a variety of reasons, for example to:

- Estimate the financial impact of the business's plans and objectives;
- Identify any need to raise additional borrowings or share capital;
- Establish working capital requirements for the forthcoming period; and
- Demonstrate the business's ability to repay borrowings or pay dividends.

A forecast is really just an updated version of a budget, reflecting actual experience during the period. The financial reality rarely plays out as anticipated in the original budget, hence the need to 'reforecast' the numbers periodically based on actual experience.

So, you need a budgeted profit & loss account and balance sheet, and a cash flow forecast – remember, cash flows and profits are not the same thing, but both are equally important.

Small business financial management

A budgeted (or forecast) profit & loss account or balance sheet looks quite like the profit & loss account and balance sheet we saw earlier, only it often goes into greater detail about individual types of income & expense/ asset & liability; and it is typically shown on a month-by month basis. Here's a template, based on a simple spreadsheet approach:

	Jan	Feb	Mar	Apr	May	Etc	Total
SALES							
Product A							
Product B							
Product C							
TOTAL SALES							
COSTS OF SALE							
Purchases							
Salaries							
Other direct costs							
TOTAL COST OF SALES							
GROSS PROFIT							
ADMIN EXPENSES							
Rent & rates							
Heat & light							
Prof fees							
Etc.							

TOTAL ADMIN EXPENSES							
OPERATING PROFIT							
Interest payable							
PROFIT BEFORE TAXATION							
Tax							
PROFIT AFTER TAXATION							

Using a spreadsheet (or even better, accounting software that can produce budgets) is a good idea, because you can produce variations on your budget to test out different "scenarios". This is also known as "sensitivity analysis" or "what if? analysis".

Testing out different scenarios as part of your budgeting process is a very good idea because it enables you to see what the financial outcome would be of different variables. For example, you can assess how your business's financial performance and position might be affected by variations in the volume of goods sold, the selling price of your goods or services, variations in your costs, investments in new fixed assets, or taking on additional borrowing.

I offer below some more suggestions about building a robust budget for the small business.

Choose the right time period

Decide what period your budget should cover, and whether it should be broken down into weeks, months, or even quarters. These questions should be decided at the outset.

Make sure the opening position is correct

Unless your business is completely starting from scratch, there will already be assets and liabilities on day one of your budget that you'll probably need to take account of, if the goal is to produce a credible, realistic budget.

Be realistic

A budget is meant to provide a realistic view of where the business is heading, against which progress can be measured, so be realistic about the assumptions made with regard to revenues, costs, spending plans etc.

Carve up your revenues by individual product/ service lines

Where your business supplies a range of products or services with very different margins or other very different characteristics, these should be recognised individually in the budget if failing to do so would result in significant inaccuracies.

Add in direct costs

Build in the direct costs of sales using assumptions that are realistic and consistent with the assumptions made elsewhere in the budget, for example about sales volumes and margins on individual lines.

Understand your margins

Understanding gross margins is key. Ensure your budget reflects sensible profit margins. We'll come back to margins shortly!

Build in seasonality

If your business is very seasonal, it makes sense to reflect that in the budget. Seasonal variations can have a major impact on profits and cash flow.

Adjust for inflation

Remember to adjust the figures for the effect of inflation and known or anticipated rises in costs. If you are striking contracts far in advance, use known figures wherever possible.

Base overheads on last year

It may be sensible to base budgeted overheads on last year's actual figures (if applicable), however do consider whether this is appropriate. If there have been major changes in circumstances, for example occupying new business premises or taking on additional back office staff, overheads may be materially different from previous years.

Include launch costs, where applicable

Remember to include your launch costs, where relevant. You may have significant costs just to get the business, or a new product, off the ground – product development, marketing etc.

Remember you'll need to pay yourself

Include your earnings, and any drawings or dividends (where applicable).

Consider the impact on revenues and costs of internal events and external factors

Think widely about what other events or factors might impact on the budgeted figures. Has the business made significant investments that should lead to improved productivity or new revenue streams? What are competitors doing and how might this affect sales volumes or pricing?

Don't forget the impact of taxation, especially VAT, PAYE and corporation tax

Taxation will have a major impact on profitability and cash flow, so the major tax impacts need to be quantified and built in.

Understand that profits and cash are not the same thing

A truly comprehensive budgeting process recognises that profits and cash flows are, almost always, not the same thing. Understanding the impact of budgeted activity on cash flows is critical for many organisations.

Build in planned investment

Whilst the temptation may be to focus on revenues and running costs, any planned investments should be factored in too; if equipment needs to be acquired, or funds need to be lent to a subsidiary company, or extra stock needs to be acquired, what will the financial impacts be?

Remember to factor in loan commitments

The business may have existing loan commitments or anticipate taking on new ones. The budgeting process should recognise such commitments and help you assess whether the business can meet continue to meet them.

Build in returns to shareholders

If dividends are planned, these should be built into the budget too. The budget would need to show that there are sufficient profits and cash available to meet planned distributions.

Do a sense check – what are the implications of your draft projections?

Having drafted your budget, it can be helpful to 'stand back' and consider the overall picture in the round. Does it stack up? What is it telling you about your plans, and do you need to adjust your strategy or be having conversations with lenders or other stakeholders? Do you need to change your whole strategy?

Reforecast periodically

Your budget provides a useful benchmark against which you can then measure actual performance. By periodically reforecasting the numbers based on actual experience, you can continue to 'look forward' and identify any further actions that may be necessary.

Use software

These days there are fantastic products available to help small business owners put this all into practice. The days of using complicated spreadsheets for budgeting purposes are, for many, becoming a thing of the past, with products like Futrli and Float offering efficient and visually appealing ways to build budgets, test scenarios and monitor actual performance. For a free demonstration of Futrli, contact me at ivan@scholesca.co.uk.

34

Profit margins

Profit margins express – in values or percentage terms – what returns a company makes on the sale of its goods or services.

Let's go back to EZCo's profit & loss account for a moment, to illustrate the point:

EZCo Ltd

Profit & loss account

For the year ended 30 April 2019

	2019	2018
	£	£
TURNOVER	150,000	60,000
Cost of sales	(80,000)	(30,000)

GROSS PROFIT	**70,000**	**30,000**
Selling and distribution costs	(5,000)	(4,000)
Administrative expenses	(30,000)	(32,000)
Other operating income	-	1,000
OPERATING PROFIT/ (LOSS)	**35,000**	**(5,000)**
Interest receivable and similar income	2,000	2,000
Interest payable and similar charges	(8,000)	-
PROFIT/ (LOSS) BEFORE TAXATION	**29,000**	**(3,000)**
Tax on profit/ (loss)	(5,000)	1,000
PROFIT/ (LOSS) FOR THE FINANCIAL YEAR	**24,000**	**(2,000)**

Gross profit

Gross profit is the return a company makes on its sales, after deducting the costs that are directly associated with producing the goods or services, but before distribution costs and other overheads.

In the above example, for 2018/19 gross profit in absolute terms is £70,000. The gross profit margin expresses the relationship between gross profit and turnover in percentage terms. £70,000 / £150,000 expressed as a percentage is 47%, so ABC Ltd has made a 47% gross profit margin in 2018/19.

To run a business successfully it's crucial to understand how profit margins work, for a number of reasons:

- When pricing your products or services you need to understand what the margins are, so that you can determine the financial consequences and understand the implications in terms of the volumes of sales that need to be achieved to cover overheads and make the target overall return;

- By understanding how margins work you can more readily understand the impact of different pricing decisions – for example the impact of a 10% discount on the top line has a very different impact on the gross profit (and indeed the net profit), depending on whether you are dealing with a relatively high or low margin product;

- By paying attention to the margins on individual product/service lines, insights can be gained into which products generate the best (and poorest) returns, which might lead to a shift in market focus, marketing activity or any other number of quite critical decisions;

- Focusing on margins may help highlight where there are cost pressures on the supply side that could indicate a need to raise prices to protect profitability;

- Profit margins can be used to compare performance trends in the business over extended time periods; they can also be used to benchmark the business against competitors or industry standards (where known).

Gross profit receives most of the attention when it comes to product pricing, but operating profit and net profit are similarly important

Operating profit

Operating profit is the return a company makes on its sales, after deducting all costs except finance costs (e.g. loan interest) and taxation. Operating profit margin expresses the relationship between operating profit and turnover in percentage terms. In the example of EZCo Ltd, operating profit is £35,000 and the operating profit margin is £35,000 / £150,000 expressed as a percentage = 23%.

Operating profit is an important measure because it explains how good the company is at turning sales into profits. For investors and creditors, this is of considerable interest. Companies need to generate sufficient operating profits to be able to provide an adequate return to investors, repay lenders and comply with the terms of any ongoing borrowing.

If operating profits do not meet expectations, business owners can interrogate further by examining turnover, the gross profit margin, and distribution costs/ administration expenses.

Net profit

Net profit is the return a company makes on its sales, after deducting finance costs. It can be calculated on profits before or after tax – it always important to be clear which of these measures is used.

The net profit margin expresses the relationship between net profits and turnover in percentage terms. In our example, net profit (after tax) is £24,000 and the net profit margin (after tax) is £24,000 / £150,000 expressed as a percentage = 16%.

Net profit is important for shareholders because their returns are based on capital growth (in the value of their shares, if there is a market for those shares) and dividends, which are financed out of the net profits of the business, after for providing for taxation.

Margin versus mark-up

One area that can cause confusion is the difference between margin and mark-up. Let's try and clear that up now!

Returning to EZCo Limited once more, as we have already seen the gross profit margin is 47%. But what about the mark-up? Mark-up expresses the amount by which a product's selling price exceeds its production cost. In our example, the average mark-up is £70,000 / £80,000 expressed as a percentage = 88%.

The relationship between margin and mark-up is *crucial* to understand when pricing your products or services:

Mark-up % = (gross profit / costs of sale) x 100

Gross Profit £ = Mark-up % x costs of sale £

Monitoring

Small business financial management

Profit margins should be closely monitored using your detailed management accounts, and corrective action should be taken on a timely basis where necessary.

Improving your margins

We'll return to the subject of pricing in a later chapter. In the meantime, consider:

- How to get your overheads down – shopping around for cheaper utilities contracts (electric, phone etc);

- Buying second hand assets, especially things like furniture and office equipment;

- Recycling consumables e.g. paper that can be printed both sides; and

- Consider bartering for products/ services – trade your goods or services for someone else's.

35

Breakeven sales quantity

Knowing your breakeven sales point is useful – often invaluable – when budgeting or forecasting your business finances. The breakeven point tells you how many sales you need to make in a given period before your business makes a profit.

Breakeven is the point your business arrives at, in any given financial period, when it makes neither a profit nor loss. To build a sustainable business, you need to make sure it breaks even in the long run – it must make profits (or at least not make losses). That is why understanding the breakeven sales quantity is valuable.

How do we work out the breakeven point? There are a few things you need to determine:

- The *sale price* of one unit of product/ service;

- The *variable cost* per unit of product/ service (those costs that vary according to the number of units produced and sold); and

- The sum of all the business's *fixed costs* (those costs that do not vary according to the number of units sold) in the period under review.

Armed with this information, you can start to work out how many sales you need to make to break even. Here's the formula:

Break even quantity = fixed costs / (sale price per unit – variable cost per unit)

Deducting the variable cost per unit from the sales price per unit gives us a figure known as the "contribution margin" - the amount in £ which each sale contributes towards your business's fixed costs.

Let's take a simple example. XYZ Ltd has budgeted for fixed costs of £50,000 for the next financial year. It sells its product, alphabet soup, at £1 per tin (it's really, really good soup!). The variable costs associated with producing each tin total £0.50. To cover its fixed costs and break even in the next financial year, it needs to sell £50,000 / (£1.00 - £0.50) = 100,000 tins.

Clearly the picture becomes more complicated if your business sells more than one product or service, each with a different contribution margin. The principals remain the same though – you just run the calculations using an appropriate "mix" of products, and you can also then see what impact different proportions of different sales categories have on the overall breakeven point.

36

Monitoring performance against budget/forecast

At this stage in the proceedings we've now covered the main tools and processes you'll need to effectively monitor and manage your business's financial performance; we've discussed management accounts; the basics of budgeting and forecasting; and some important concepts around profit margins and breakeven sales.

As the business owner, on a regular basis - at least quarterly - you should be aiming to:

- Review detailed management accounts (profit & loss account and balance sheet) and interpret what has happened in terms of the business's financial performance and position;

- Review the impact of any major actions recently taken;
- Compare the actual financial performance and position to the budget;
- Prepare or update the forecast profit & loss account and balance sheet, if required;
- Prepare or update the cash flow forecast, if required; and
- Take any corrective action that is necessary within the business, in light of the information reviewed.

If your underlying financial processes and procedures are operating as they should, your reviews should be mainly about figuring out what to do with your business - not about identifying errors in the information! But if you do spot any errors in the information at this stage, take the time to sort them out.

The next chapter "Common problems with management accounts" discusses some of the most common errors I see with management information.

Reviewing your management accounts – getting started

Anyway, back to your review of the management accounts. If you're still struggling to know where to start with this, here are some suggestions to get you going. A "ten-point plan", if you will.

1. Gather up your management accounts, those for the prior period, and your budget or forecast.

Monitoring performance against budget/ forecast

2. Get yourself a pen and paper, pc, laptop or mobile device to make notes.

3. Starting with the profit & loss account, start from the top and work your way down, noting as you go:

    a. Turnover – and how it compares to the prior period and to your budget or forecast.

    b. Gross profit – note the gross profit and gross profit margin, and how they compare to prior period/ budget.

    c. Gross profit margin – did your business make the margin it expected to, on the sales that it made.

    d. Selling and distribution costs – and how they compare to prior period/ budget.

    e. Administrative overheads – and how they compare to prior period/ budget.

    f. Operating profit – note your operating profit and operating profit margin, and compare to the prior period/ budget.

    g. Interest receivable – note any investment income and consider whether it reflects the returns you were expecting your business to make on any investments held.

- h. Interest payable – note any interest expense and consider whether it is consistent with the cost you would expect in relation to any borrowing.

- i. Profit before tax – note the profit before tax and net profit margin, and compare to the prior period/ budget.

- j. Taxation – is the tax charge consistent with your understanding of the tax the business would pay on the profits made in the period to date?

4. Review the notes you made and highlight any points that you think require further investigation or attention. At the end of your "initial review" you'll come back to these points and investigate further as necessary by interrogating the data in your accounting records in more detail to see what's going on.

5. Next, get your balance sheet. Starting at the top and again making notes as you go, look at:

    - a. Fixed assets – do these fully reflect all the fixed assets your business owns? Compare to the figures in the prior period and consider if any change in the amount is consistent with your expectations – for example did you buy or sell any assets in the latest period; has depreciation been correctly applied?

    - b. Stock – does the stock figure represent the cost (or, if lower, net realisable value) of stock held at the end of the period? Is the business holding an appropriate amount of stock to meet demand, but not over stocking (and tying up capital) or under stocking (and risking running out)?

c. Debtors – what is your business owed, how does this compare with the prior period/ budget, is this consistent with your expectations, and are there any overdue amounts that need to be pursued?

d. Bank – how much money is held in the bank account, and could this indicate a potential cash flow problem down the road? Alternatively, is there a surplus of cash that could be reinvested into the business or distributed to shareholders?

e. Creditors – what does your business owe, how does this compare with the prior period/ budget, is this consistent with your expectations, and are there any amounts that are overdue that could lead to trouble?

f. Net current assets – look at the business's net current assets (current assets less current liabilities) and compare the position to the prior period and to the budget/ forecast. If the value of net current assets is falling – or if there are net current liabilities – this could indicate an impending liquidity problem, in other words the business may struggle to pay its bills on time.

g. Provisions for liabilities – when a business needs to show a liability in the accounts but the amount can only be estimated, it may create a provision. Consider if any provisions are reasonable and reflect the best available estimate of likely cost.

h. Net assets – review the net assets value (the total of all assets less all liabilities). If it's a negative number, your business may be technically insolvent!

i. Capital and reserves – review the capital and reserves balances. If the balance on the retained profits account is negative, your business will not be allowed to pay dividends, since dividends may only be paid out of retained profits.

6. Again, review the notes you made about the balance sheet and highlight any that you think require further investigation or attention. At the end of your "initial review" you'll come back to these points and investigate further as necessary by interrogating the data in your accounting records in more detail to see what's going on.

7. Consider what impact any recent events might have had on the figures you're looked at. These might be internal events (e.g. a price rise, a new product launch, a machinery breakdown), or external events (e.g. supplier price rises, a new competitor, or regulatory changes). Make additional notes as required.

Monitoring performance against budget/ forecast

8. Now go ahead and follow up your detailed notes about the profit & loss account and balance sheet, making sure you understand what's going on - and record any changes you need to make in the business as a result of the issues you have identified.

9. Consider if you need to update the budget or forecast based on the "actual" financial results and any changes you now intend to make in the business. If so, do that now.

10. Consider if you need to prepare a new cash flow forecast to check that your business will have sufficient cash for the forthcoming month or quarter. If so, do it now.

You may also want to produce some Key Performance Indicators (KPI's) alongside your management accounts to help you monitor your business's performance and position. We'll come back to KPI's shortly.

37

Common problems with management accounts

I hope the following list of common problems with management accounts may help you avoid some of the pitfalls. In the course of my work with Scholes CA I often help small businesses resolve these sorts of problems – hopefully by writing this book I'll help you avoid the same mistakes!

Incorrectly categorising expenses

Expenses may be categorised incorrectly. A very common example concerns capital expenditure that has been posted to profit & loss. As a general rule, if a company is buying tangible items for long-term use within the business, the cost goes to the balance sheet as a fixed asset, not to the profit & loss account.

Remedy: take care when posting expenditure and ask your accountant if in any doubt about the classification of a particular item.

Putting personal expenses through the books

Companies have separate "legal personality" to the owners/ employees, so personal transactions should generally be kept completely separate from the business. Where a company settles a personal liability, there will often be tax / NIC consequences for both the company and the individual, so it is sensible to seek advice when in doubt.

Remedy: keep personal transactions separate; if it is proposed to put personal transactions through the books, seek advice as to any potential tax implications.

Not dealing with cut off correctly

Accounts prepared on the "accruals basis" are supposed to show the economic effects of a business's activity, rather than simple cash flows (which on their own rarely tell the whole story, and can be very misleading).

When preparing quality management accounts we therefore need to think about, and potentially adjust the figures for, "cut off" issues, for example:

- Income earned in the period that hasn't yet been invoiced to customers;
- Income invoiced in the period that hasn't yet been earned;

- Expenses incurred in the period that haven't yet been invoiced to the business;
- Expense invoices/ payments in the period for benefits that extend beyond the period end; and
- The effect of stock movements around the period end.

Although these concepts may be regarded as part of the accountant's "black art", the truth is they are very important in making sure your management accounts reflect what is actually going on in economic terms, rather than some alternate reality (aka nonsense).

Remedy: consider the impact of cut-off and ask your accountant for advice if unsure.

Not adjusting for movements in stock and work in progress

Businesses whose stock fluctuates significantly from one period to the next need to make sure the management accounts take into account those movements. Without doing so, the cost of sales and gross profit information presented in management accounts may be very misleading.

Remedy: include significant stock movements in the periodic management accounts.

Not posting depreciation

In asset-intensive businesses, depreciation will often be a significant cost component in the statutory accounts. If the objective is to produce management accounts which are broadly in line with the year-end, statutory accounts, then depreciation should be accounted for in-year.

For example, if you want to work out how much dividend can be paid out without exhausting reserves, depreciation (as well as other things like corporation tax) must be factored in.

Remedy: include depreciation in the management accounts; this may be based on the details in the business's fixed asset register (if you or your accountant maintains one).

Duplicating expenses

I sometimes see businesses posting supplier invoices into the purchase ledger; then, when the invoice is subsequently paid, the payment is posted straight to the profit & loss account. If the business is VAT registered, this may result in input VAT being overclaimed (as well as making the management accounts incorrect!).

Remedy: ensure that invoice payments are posted against the relevant supplier invoice, instead of being posted directly to the profit & loss account.

Tip: periodic reviews of the aged creditors report can point to a problem in this area - if the report contains loads of old creditor balances that you think have been paid, then it usually points to one of two things, either the payment has been posted straight to the profit & loss account; or the supplier was paid by the owner, or perhaps in cash (instead of from the business's bank account).

Not operating basic financial controls properly

Reconciling the bank account and other key control accounts (wages, PAYE, pension, VAT) periodically - and *following up and resolving* any problems - is a basic financial discipline that all bookkeepers should master. It may seem boring, but it's important because it gives you a degree of comfort that the information coming out of the system is reliable and not rubbish!

Remedy: regularly reconcile all key control accounts and investigate and resolve any discrepancies on a timely basis. If you don't know how to do this, ask your accountant for help.

38

Key performance indicators

We've already looked at how management accounts, budgets and cash flow forecasts can provide you with lots of useful financial information to help you stay in control.

The trouble is, you're a busy person and you don't always have time to read all this stuff. What's the answer? Can all this information be distilled down into a few, simple but all-important measures? Why yes - it probably can!

With good quality, timely management information it should be possible to define and measure some "Financial Key Performance Indicators" (KPI's) that can help you monitor and measure the performance and status of the most important areas of your business.

KPI's can be used for a variety of purposes; tracking your business's performance against plan is perhaps the most obvious one, but they may also be used to identify emerging trends or to benchmark your business against competitors or industry standards.

Some KPI's to get you started

There is a very wide range of KPI's from which to choose; it is therefore important to carefully select measures according to the type of business you run and your unique objectives. A good accountant should be able to help you select and apply the right KPI's for your business. However, to get you started here is a selection of some of the most common financial KPI's:

1. Gross profit margin

Gross profit margin can indicate whether you are pricing your goods or services correctly. As we have already seen, the calculation is (gross profit / sales), expressed as a percentage. Gross profits should be sufficient to cover fixed overheads and leave you with a profit.

2. Net profit margin

The net profit is the bottom line, after deducting all expenses, including corporation tax if your business is a company. The net profit margin is calculated as (net profit / sales), expressed as a percentage. If you have a sole trade or partnership business, net profits need to be enough to cover your personal needs (including your personal tax liabilities), with sufficient capital left in the business to fund ongoing trading.

3. Aged debtors

If your business makes sales on credit terms, track your aged debtors. This means quantifying the amount owed within and outwith normal payment terms, the objective being to minimise (or preferably eliminate) any overdue amounts. It is commonplace to split aged debtors into amounts due in under 30 days, 30 to 60 days, and over 60/ over 90 days, though you may wish to tailor the ageing according to your own requirements.

4. Working capital

Working capital ratios provide an indication of your business's ability to pay the bills as they fall due. Perhaps the best known example is the current ratio, calculated as (current assets / current liabilities), expressed as a number. A number below 1 may strongly suggest that the business has insufficient cash to pay the bills on time. We'll get into ratios in more detail shortly.

Choosing KPI's for your business

When deciding what KPI's to use, consider what areas:

- Are *critical* to your cash flows, sales and profits;
- Relate to competitive advantages enjoyed by your business;
- Are high risk - which areas are most likely to go wrong?

For each KPI, you want to determine a target. Targets should be clear, relevant, measureable and achievable. The point of establishing targets is:

- So you can track actual performance against your business plan/ budget; and
- To help communicate to staff the *crucial* performance measures they need to focus on.

It is also helpful to identify comparator values (e.g. from the prior period) so that performance *trends* can be established for individual KPI's - is the performance getting better or worse compared to the prior reporting period?

Your KPI's should be both financial and non-financial; simple, easy to measure and understand; outward-looking; generally long-term focused; and consistently measured and reported. Consider what KPI's you might wish to establish in each of the following areas:

- Strategic - business growth, response to developments in the market, research & development;
- Financial - profits, cash flows, liquidity, stability;
- People - training and development, welfare, productivity;
- Operational - production efficiency, wastage;
- Marketing & sales - return on investment from sales and marketing activities; and
- Customer relationships - customer satisfaction, customer loyalty.

KPI's on their own have no intrinsic value. So once you've established your KPI's, you then need a routine to monitor - and communicate to relevant managers and staff - how the business is actually performing against the KPI's. This is the important bit that can get overlooked. It is only by *acting on the information provided* (to address any issues or capitalise on opportunities identified) that the business will derive any value from the whole process.

39

How ratio analysis can help you manage the finances

So, we've covered in some depth how you can (should!) regularly produce and review management accounts and KPI's to check your business's financial performance and position. Hopefully you've now got a pretty good grip on how this will help you stay in control of the finances and make better decisions. But - we can do better yet!

When you are reviewing your management accounts or establishing KPI's, a set of techniques known as "ratio analysis" can help you build an even deeper understanding of your business finances. Please don't be put off by the title; ratio analysis is not some complex mathematical approach beyond the understanding of the ordinary mortal; in fact, it requires no more than a very basic grasp of maths.

Ratio analysis offers us a way to be able to:

- More confidently manage the profitability, liquidity, gearing and stability of your business;
- Make better decisions by understanding the financial consequences of the actions that you take;
- Understand more deeply the relationship between the financial performance and position of your business;
- Track changes in the financial performance and position of the business over time;
- Objectively compare your business against competitors and against industry norms; and
- Understand how your business may be seen (and judged!) by external parties such as credit rating agencies, competitors, suppliers and customers.

We are concerned here primarily with *financial management ratios*. There is also a set of ratios known as *investment ratios*, which we'll not be getting into here!

Anyway, it's convenient to group financial management ratios into two categories: financial performance ratios; and financial position ratios.

Financial performance ratios tell us about how well the business performs in financial terms. These are further sub-divided into:

- Profitability ratios, which are concerned with how profitable the business is; and
- Efficiency ratios, which are concerned with the business's ability to generate sales income from the resources it uses.

One of the most important financial performance measures – perhaps *the* most - is "return on capital employed", or ROCE for short. All of the other profitability and efficiency ratios discussed in the following chapter impact on ROCE in one way or another.

Financial position ratios tell us about the financial status of a business at a point in time. These are further subdivided into:

- Liquidity ratios, which shine a light onto a business's ability to meet short term financial commitments; and
- Stability ratios, which provide an indication of the sustainability of a business's financial arrangements.

Performance ratios are key to increasing the perceived value of your business to lenders, investors and suppliers; position ratios are important to manage as they might impact your business's credit worthiness or ability to borrow.

Let's get into each of the sub-groups in a little more detail...

40

Financial performance ratios

In this chapter we'll consider financial performance ratios, which help you interpret your business's profitability and efficiency – and the link between the two.

Profitability ratios

Profitability ratios tell us something about how well your business generates profits from its resources and revenues. Sustainable improvements in your profitability ratios over time will help to increase the value of your business.

Here are the key profitability ratios:

1. Return on capital employed (operating profit / (total assets – current liabilities))

This tells us how well the business uses its capital to generate profits. It's arguably the most important measure of all as it tells us about the business's ability to generate value.

Return on capital employed is impacted by each of the other measures of profitability...

2. Operating margin (operating profit / turnover)

    This tells us how well the business turns sales into operating profits.

3. Gross margin (gross profit / turnover)

    This tells us how well the business converts sales into gross profits

4. Operating expenses to sales (operating expenses / turnover)

    This tells us the proportion of sales revenue consumed by operating expenses

Operating margins can be improved by increasing the gross margin or reducing the operating expenses to sales ratio. Consider what opportunities exist in your business:

- to increase the gross margin by improving the relationship between your sales price and the costs associated with making or buying the products you sell, or providing the service you sell;

- to reduce the operating expenses to sales ratio by better management of the costs associated with distribution, selling and administrative activities within your business.

Efficiency ratios

Efficiency ratios tell us something about how well your business generates revenues from its resources. Your business's return on capital employed is affected by efficiency ratios as well as by its operating profit margin.

Sustainable improvements in your efficiency ratios over time will also therefore help to increase the profitability (and hence the value) of your business.

Here are the key efficiency ratios:

1. Turnover on capital employed (turnover / (total assets − current liabilities)

   How well has the business used capital to generate sales?

2. Turnover on fixed assets (turnover / fixed assets)

   How well does the business generate revenue from its investment in fixed assets?

3. Turnover on working capital (turnover / net current assets)

   How well does the business generate revenue from its investment in working capital?

4. Stock days (stock x 365) / cost of sales

How many days of cost of sales are represented by year end stock?

5. Debtor days (debtors x 365) / turnover

    How many days of sales are represented by year end debtors?

6. Creditor days (creditors x 365) / cost of sales

    How many days of cost of sales are represented by year end creditors?

Stock, debtor and creditor days are sometimes known as the "working capital ratios". What do we mean by "working capital"?

Working capital and the cash conversion cycle

Working capital is the name given to the financial resources used by a business to fund its day-to-day trading activities. It tells us how much *liquidity* a business has – whether the business has enough resources to be able to pay its bills on time – and is calculated using this formula:

Working capital = current assets - current liabilities

Remember, current assets are those assets that can be turned into cash relatively quickly – stock, trade debtors – or which are already cash! Current liabilities are those liabilities that will fall due in the short term, within the next year.

Here's the point: if a business has insufficient working capital, it will be unable to pay its liabilities as they fall due, and may as a result fail. Please understand that even very profitable businesses can experience working capital problems – so you need to be laser-focused on managing your business's working capital *at all times*.

The *working capital cycle* (or cash conversion cycle) is a related concept which shows the amount of time it takes a business to turn net current assets into cash. A simple example: a business that pays its suppliers in 30 days, but takes 45 days to get paid by its customers, has a working capital cycle of 15 days. The cycle is usually funded with the business's cash reserves - or a bank overdraft. And since an overdraft costs money, this is another good reason to reduce the working capital cycle as far as possible.

Managing your business's working capital requires a focus on all of the following:

- Retaining (if possible) sufficient cash to fund the working capital cycle;

- Keeping stocks at the optimum level to permit uninterrupted production and sales, but without over-stocking (since that ties up cash and resources unnecessarily);

- Collecting amounts due from debtors as promptly as possible; potentially reducing the amount of credit offered to customers, or getting paid earlier on in the sales process;

- Negotiating credit with suppliers and taking advantage of available credit; and finally,

- Securing short-term finance to cover any shortfall in working capital, once the above steps have been considered – for example a bank overdraft or invoice finance.

Businesses generally aim to keep working capital as low as possible and some are even able to sustain a negative working capital position. Improving the working capital management ratios will reduce the amount of external finance needed to support the growth of your business, so the incentive is clear.

We'll return to the subject of working capital management shortly.

The relationship between profitability and efficiency

There is a direct relationship between profitability and efficiency, expressed through the return on capital employed (ROCE).

- ROCE = operating profit / (total assets − current liabilities);
- Operating profit margin = operating profit / turnover;
- Turnover on capital employed = turnover / (total assets − current liabilities).

ROCE is driven by two things: the revenue generated using the business's capital (which is a measure of efficiency); and the operating profit (which is a measure of profitability). Your business's ROCE can be improved by being generating more turnover with the business's capital ("sweating the assets"), by improving profitability, or both.

Exercise

If you're feeling bold, it's time to put some of this stuff into practice!

Grab your last set of accounts now – it doesn't really matter if it's the statutory accounts or more recent management accounts – a pen, paper and calculator.

Then, work out the profitability and efficiency ratios above, for the current *and comparative* periods. Compare the two, refer to the notes above, and see if you notice anything interesting. I hope this shines a little light on at least one or two aspects of your business's finances.

41

Financial position ratios

In this chapter we'll return to financial position ratios, which tell you about your business's liquidity and financial stability.

Liquidity ratios

How well can your business meet its short term obligations? Liquidity ratios impact on the perceived 'credit worthiness' of a business and therefore can impact the ability to get credit from suppliers or borrow from lenders.

1. Current ratio (current assets / current liabilities)

    How well can the business meet its short term obligations from current assets?

2. Quick ratio (current assets excl. stock / current liabilities)

How well can the business meet its short term obligations from liquid current assets?

Liquidity can be improved through better management of working capital, as discussed in the last chapter.

Stability ratios

How well can the business meet its longer-term obligations?

Stability ratios are used by lenders to assess a business's ability to manage its borrowings. Lenders often stipulate 'threshold values' for these ratios which are contractual requirements or 'covenants' built into loan agreements.

1. Gearing ratio (debt x 100) / (debt + share capital & reserves)

   What proportion of total finance does debt represent?

2. Interest cover (operating profit / net interest payable)

   How easily can the business cover its interest charges from operating profits?

An increase in gearing has two main effects; it increases financial risk; and it magnifies returns on shareholders' funds (and indeed losses).

Increases in gearing can help finance growth, but if the level of borrowing is perceived to be too high, creating too much risk, what can be done? Options might include introducing more share capital; reducing dividends; or deferring major capital investments.

Exercise

It's time to put some of this stuff into practice once again!

Grab your last set of accounts now – it doesn't really matter if it's the statutory accounts or more recent management accounts – a pen, paper and calculator.

Then, work out the liquidity and stability ratios above, for the current *and comparative* periods. Compare the two, refer to the notes above, and see if you notice anything interesting. One thing to mention – if your business has no borrowings, the stability ratios won't work – just ignore them!

42

Managing your working capital

One of the keys to successful financial management is effective working capital management. Put simply, working capital is the net amount of liquid assets at the business's disposal - debtors, stock, and cash, less short-term liabilities like trade creditors and taxes. It's a measure of the business's overall liquidity, efficiency and financial health. And managing this effectively is key to improving a business's ability to grow, without recourse to more expensive, external sources of finance.

There is sometimes scope for the small business to improve its working capital position through quite simple and inexpensive measures. Occasionally, the results can even be dramatic. Here are my top tips for effective working capital management:

1. Make sure you get paid on time, every time. Assess the credit risks that come with new customers. Be clear about your payment terms. Consider if your terms could be improved; could customers pay up front? Monitor your debtors; chase the late payers; have a system to escalate in cases of persistent non-payment.

2. Don't overstock. Money tied up in stock cannot be put to use elsewhere. Manage your stock levels; understand what's shifting and what isn't; manage your supply chain and apply 'just in time' principles.

3. Make sure money in the business is working hard for you. If your business has excessive funds in the bank earning very little return, ask if this is the best use of the money. Could it be invested elsewhere for a better return?

4. Negotiate better credit terms with your suppliers; and take advantage of the terms you agree. If you pay your suppliers on presentation of invoice, but your customers take 60 days to pay you... there may be a problem. Remember the working capital cycle!

5. Negotiate favourable terms for your bank credit facility. If your business does require an overdraft to support its working capital requirements, make sure you aren't paying over the odds.

In a world where many small businesses are still struggling to get the finance they need to grow, it's essential to explore all the options.

Working capital management - getting one's own house in order - is a great place to start. Charity, as they say, begins at home.

43

Cash flow crisis management

Even very profitable businesses can experience cash flow problems from time to time, especially in periods of growth. So, what to do in a cash flow crisis?

I thought it would be helpful at this stage to spell out the things a business needs to do when faced with a cash flow *crisis*. If everything we've spoken about so far hasn't helped. If something unexpected has thrown things off track. I'm talking about the stuff you might need to do *right now*. Here we go...

Extend supplier credit terms

Why not get on the phone to your suppliers and ask for them to extend their normal credit terms? They won't all agree to it, but some probably will, especially if you have good relationships and a long history.

Sell underused plant & equipment

Look at the plant & machinery, vehicles, office equipment you have. Is it all being used? Consider selling the things that are redundant or underused. Would leasing, rather than owning some assets help cash flow in the short run?

Sell stock

Look at any stock your business is holding. Could some of this be turned into cash relatively quickly, perhaps by cutting prices (OK, that's a short term fix but we are talking about a *crisis* here)? Is there obsolete stock that could be turned into cash, one way or another? Is there any unpaid stock that is unlikely to sell quickly, that can be returned to suppliers now?

Review work-in-progress

Review your work-in-progress and identify any work that can be billed to customers now. And bill them now! Continue to bill any further work in progress as promptly and frequently as possible.

Renegotiate customer invoicing and credit terms

Can you renegotiate the invoicing / credit terms offered to customers, so that work is billed earlier/ more frequently, and credit terms are less generous? If not for existing contracts, then at least for any new ones?

Chase debtors, especially overdue ones

Which customers owe your business money? Are there any that are overdue? Can you get on the phone and chase them for payment? Escalate recovery action if necessary (hopefully it won't be necessary!).

Tax bills not yet due? Negotiate "time to pay"

If your business has some tax bills that are not yet due for payment, it's possible to negotiate "time to pay" arrangements with HMRC. This is best done before the payment due date.

If tax bills are already overdue for payment, get your accountant to speak with HMRC and explain the situation anyway, it's less likely they will appoint debt collectors if they know the score.

Cut (or delay) unnecessary expenditure

Go through your budget line by line. Identify any expenditure that can be i) delayed or ii) cut altogether, without adversely affecting the business's trading activities. Delay or cut that expenditure.

Speak to the bank

For obvious reasons, probably the very worst time to speak to the bank is when your business is already in the midst of a cash flow crisis. But it is an option.

Can an extension to the overdraft be negotiated? Will additional security need to be put up? Will a more fundamental review of the business's financing arrangements (borrowing and equity) be required, once the current crisis has been dealt with?

Raise funds personally

Can you raise funds to provide some short term cash for the business? This can be a risky strategy (since you might not get your money back, if the short term cash flow problems turn into long term problems), but sometimes it's necessary, especially if the measures above are insufficient and the bank is unwilling to help.

OK, that's enough cash flow chat! Let's now move on to sunnier climes...

44

The value of pre year-end planning

The weeks leading up to the end of your business's financial year can be a very good time for you to stand back, take stock, and perhaps take some additional actions on the financial front.

With appropriate planning, you may be able to make financial decisions in the run up to the year end knowing, with a high degree of confidence, what the consequences will be – for the accounts, and for the associated corporation tax or income tax liabilities. In other words you may be able to influence – entirely legitimately, I must add - how the accounts look, and what the tax bill will be.

Do also bear in mind that your accounts may be read far and wide – not only by the tax authorities, but also, potentially, by lenders, credit ratings agencies, suppliers, and so on. People that matter. So it is useful to be thinking in advance of the year end about the impression your accounts might make on third parties.

Here's the big point though: the timing of all this is crucial. Once the year-end is by with, there are far fewer options available. There is far less "wriggle room" (in fact there is none, basically). So, when it comes to organising a company's finances, take the opportunity to consider if there is anything else you need to do on the financial front *in the weeks leading up to the year end.*

Reasons to plan pre year-end

What sort of pre year-end planning measures might you wish to consider? It depends to some extent on what your goals are, so that's a good starting point. For example, are you looking to:

- Minimise, legitimately, the corporation tax/ income tax bill?
- Present a strong balance sheet for lenders?
- Present good earnings levels to secure personal borrowing?
- Secure R&D tax credits?
- Demonstrate a track record of growth, with a view to 'selling up' or attracting outside investment?

These are just a few examples of the different motivations that might drive pre year-end planning activities (they are not mutually exclusive, either).

Although specific planning measures will be unique to each individual business, it is possible to group together some of the more common ones. Here they are:

Influencing the timing of transactions

In some cases it may be possible (and desirable) to influence the timing of sales, either bringing forward, or delaying, when sales are made in order to impact the business's reported turnover and assets.

Perhaps more frequently, businesses accelerate or delay discretionary spend in various areas, for example replacement plant & machinery; repairs, advertising, training, or product development.

If your business is structured as a limited company, the timing and amount of directors' remuneration and dividends can also be relatively easy to control and adjust according to circumstances.

The main benefit of controlling the timing of transactions is usually the cash flow benefit of delaying when corporation tax/ income tax is paid.

Research & Development

Companies that undertake qualifying research & development projects can receive extra tax breaks under the R&D Tax Credits Scheme.

Where there is R&D activity that may be eligible for R&D tax credits, care should be taken to structure the activities to maximise entitlement to the relief.

Profit extraction policy

Directors of smaller companies often have significant or even total control over how profits are extracted. The profit extraction approach should be reviewed periodically - and whenever there is any major change in circumstances - to ensure that it remains optimal, in terms of tax efficiency and the financial impact on the company and the individuals. Normally here, we are looking at a variety of issues, including:

- Salary & bonuses;
- Benefits in kind;
- Employer pension contributions;
- Dividends; and
- Directors' loans.

Generally you should avoid borrowing money from your company – in other words having an overdrawn director's loan account – since there can be punitive tax consequences.

That said, in certain circumstances it can be sensible (even desirable) to borrow money from your company - but mostly only for short periods of time, with any loans being repaid on a permanent basis within nine months of the financial year end.

Read my blog about directors' loan accounts at www.scholesca.co.uk/blog/directors-loan-accounts.

Audit

Consideration may need to be given to whether a statutory audit may be required; or, if not required, whether a voluntary audit would be desirable.

Accounting policies

Your business's accounting policies should be kept under review, not only to ensure they remain prudent and commercially correct, but also to see that they are congruent with the business's overall financial aims.

For example, what are the policies for:

- Income recognition?
- Expensing or capitalising R&D costs?
- Recognising fixed assets at valuation, or depreciated historic cost?
- Fixed asset depreciation rates, useful lives and residual values?
- Stock valuation?
- Recognising bad debts, obsolete stock, warranty costs etc?

Business model

It may be appropriate to review the financial/ business model, for example:

- Relationships with associated businesses - e.g. management charges, group tax reliefs;

- Altering the year end to capture or exclude good/ not-so-good periods of trading;
- Restructuring borrowings and share capital;
- Restructuring personal borrowing to maximise tax relief; and
- Considering if an alternative business structure (company/ sole trade/ partnership) would be preferable.

We'll return to the subject of business structures in part 4.

Balance sheet

Finally, with pre year end planning there may be a temptation to focus heavily on the profit & loss account (sales, margins etc), but the balance sheet should not be overlooked.

Consider what can be done to improve the working capital ratios and reduce gearing. Also, if you're running a company, don't forget to consider repaying any overdrawn directors' loan accounts.

For a free pre year end planning factsheet, email me at ivan@scholesca.co.uk.

45

Strengthening the balance sheet

When thinking about your business's finances, often all the focus seems to be on the profit & loss account. As we've already seen, this is only part of the picture.

The balance sheet reveals significant information about the state of financial health of a small business – and if you run a company, often it's only the balance sheet that appears on the public record, as most small companies take advantage of available filing exemptions to limit what gets filed at Companies House.

The balance sheet is also of particular interest to credit ratings agencies, banks and other lenders. In assessing the creditworthiness of a business, these operators pay close attention to what the balance sheet is saying.

It therefore makes sense for you to actively consider what can be done to strengthen and improve your business's balance sheet. I offer a few suggestions below.

Revalue assets

In most circumstances, the default position in small business's financial statements is that fixed assets are shown at their historic cost, less accumulated depreciation. It is, however, permissible to show assets like land & buildings at "fair value" - basically their open market value.

If some of the fixed assets on your business's balance sheet were bought some time ago, their depreciated historic cost may bear no relation at all to their current market value. Revaluing such assets in an upward direction improves the strength of the balance sheet by increasing asset values.

Sell unproductive assets

If your business is holding onto underperforming assets - little-used plant or obsolete stock, for example - then it may be time to dispose of those items and reinvest into something that will provide a better return.

Capitalise intangible assets

Expenditure on intangible assets may be capitalised in certain circumstances. The alternative, expensing the cost through the profit & loss account, will by comparison result in lower reported profits (or increased losses). Potential examples include expenditure on software; property leases; goodwill; patents; trademarks; and some development costs.

Monitor and manage working capital

Careful attention to the working capital position can strengthen the balance sheet. We discussed all that earlier on – but it's really important so worth another mention here!

Manage the timing of discretionary expenditure

Profit & loss accounts cover a span of time (normally a year); balance sheets, by contrast, are like a financial "snapshot" taken on one specific day. If your business has discretion over the timing of certain expenditure, consider when the best time would be to incur that expenditure?

By delaying revenue expenditure until a subsequent financial year (which, if you are approaching the year-end, may mean a delay of only a few days or weeks), the strength of the balance sheet - not to mention the current year's profits - may be improved.

Deferred tax assets

If you run a company that has trading losses available to carry forward against future years' profits, these normally represent value for the company as they can effectively help reduce future tax bills.

Where it is more likely than not that those losses will be relieved in future periods, a deferred tax asset may be recognised in the balance sheet, improving the company's net asset value.

Convert debt to equity

It's not unusual for director/ shareholders to lend significant sums of money to their small companies, often on a long term basis.

In some circumstances it is possible to convert such debt into equity shares, and in so doing remove the debt from the balance sheet without creating a tax charge for the company - or the lender. The money can still potentially be repaid at a future point when funds permit, for example through a share buyback.

Issue new shares

Another one for the limited company owners in the room: in some cases there may be the possibility of further equity investment, either from existing shareholders and/ or other parties. More share capital equates to a stronger balance sheet.

Care must be taken however not to fall foul of the Financial Conduct Authority's regulations concerning financial promotions. The implications of potential changes in control or dilution of control also must be borne in mind. Take professional advice before proceeding!

46

Dividends – getting the details right

A dividend is a payment a company can make to its shareholders out of the profits it has made.

It is not a cost of business, so it won't appear as an "expense" in the profit & loss account - rather, it is a distribution of profits, which reduces shareholders' equity.

Where the shares in issue are all of the same class, each shareholder will normally receive a dividend in proportion to the number of shares they hold.

Declaring a dividend

To pay a dividend, the directors of the company normally hold a meeting to "declare" the dividend; a minute of the meeting should be retained.

Retained profits and illegal dividends

Companies are not allowed to pay a dividend in excess of "distributable profits". This sounds complex, but the concept is pretty simple really. All it means is that a company cannot pay out a dividend in excess of the profits that it has made (and not already paid out).

Think of "distributable profits" as a piggy bank - when the company makes a profit (after allowing for corporation tax), it tops up the balance in the piggy bank - when it pays out a dividend, it reduces it again. The key figure to watch is the "retained profits" figure in the balance sheet.

When making a decision about declaring a dividend part-way through a financial year, if there is any doubt whether there are sufficient distributable profits available, reliable and up-to-date management accounts will be needed to confirm the position, before a final decision is made.

Paperwork

When a dividend is to be paid, a dividend voucher should be prepared for each shareholder showing the:

- Company name;
- Date;
- Shareholder's name; and
- Amount of the dividend.

Each shareholder should be given a dividend voucher, and the company should retain a copy for its own records.

For a free dividend voucher template, email me at ivan@scholesca.co.uk.

Taxation

The shareholders may be liable to pay income tax on any dividends received. Dividend income is declared on the individual's Self Assessment tax return. UK taxpayers can receive up to £2,000 in dividend income (in 2019/20) without paying income tax, but dividend income above that level is subject to income tax at rates of 7.5%, 32.5% or 38.1%, depending on the taxpayer's other taxable income in the tax year.

The payment of a dividend is not a taxable deduction for the company (again, because it is a distribution of profits, not a business expense).

PART 4

MAKING BIG FINANCIAL DECISIONS

47

First, select your team

We've covered all the basics in parts 1 to 3, from basic financial procedures through understanding the accounts to using those accounts to actively manage your business finances.

In this final section of the book we'll examine in a bit more detail some of the big financial decisions that small business owners may need to make at various stages in in the "business lifecycle".

With any big financial decision, probably the first thing you should do is pull the right team together – your lawyer, accountant, financial adviser – in fact whoever has the right expertise to help you reach a good decision.

On many occasions I have seen small business owners try to "muddle through" big decisions alone, when they really, *really* would have benefited from proper professional advice. This usually comes down to trying to save money on professional fees.

Whilst I can understand the motivation to keep professional costs down, I rather like the old adage "if you think the professionals are expensive, wait until you hire an amateur". I think that's very apt, especially where major financial decisions are concerned.

48

Choosing a business structure

If you are thinking about setting up a business or going self-employed, one of your key considerations should be your business structure. Popular ways to set up your business include: sole trader; partnership; and company. The structure you choose should depend on careful consideration of your goals and circumstances, including:

- The size of your business;
- How much profits (or, in the short term, losses) you expect to make;
- How much risk you are prepared to accept;
- Your other income; and
- Whether you have family you can involve.

Even if your business is already up and running, you should periodically revisit this topic because if circumstances change then altering the current structure of your business may be appropriate.

We'll now examine the most common structures adopted by small businesses in the UK, starting with...

Sole traders

A sole trader, as the name suggests, is where you are set up on your own and is the simplest structure.

This may suit a small, simple business, with relatively low income levels (perhaps below the higher income tax thresholds). Common examples of people who set up as sole traders include 'one man band' businesses such as folk involved in the construction industry who want to be self-employed. Generally the set-up costs of sole traders are low, compared to companies and partnerships.

As a sole trader, you keep all of your profits and are in sole control of establishing and running the business, however a big downside is that you have unlimited liability. Unlimited liability means that your personal assets may be used to pay off any business debts! With a sole trade you may also have less flexibility in tax planning opportunities, compared to a partnership or company structure.

Partnerships

A partnership is a structure where you and at least one other person combine to run a business together. A partnership agreement is commonly created to define who is involved, profit sharing, and

Choosing a business structure

salaries, and this can make it more expensive and complex to set up than a sole trade.

In a partnership, profits can be shared in whatever proportions the partners agree, as stated in the partnership agreement. This may provide opportunities to apportion profits tax effectively! Like a sole trader, each partner in an ordinary partnership has unlimited liability, meaning that any partner's personal assets may be used to pay off any business debts.

People often set up partnerships to include their spouse or adult children. This allows more flexibility in sharing profits and managing personal tax arrangements. For example, profit sharing arrangements may be structured in a way that utilises a partner's unused income tax personal allowance or basic rate tax band. As long as this reflects each individual partner's economic contribution to the business, this is perfectly fine. This type of arrangement can be especially beneficial to businesses with significant profits, or where some partners have exposure to higher income tax rates.

Maintaining good relations between partners in a partnership is very important. Conflicts arising between partners, whether it be a family partnership or a purely business relationship, could have a knock-on effect on the business's performance, or even lead to an expensive break-up of the business, therefore trust is essential to effective partnership working.

Limited liability partnerships (LLP's) may be a useful alternative to ordinary partnerships where partners wish to limit their financial exposure whilst still benefiting from the flexible nature this type of structure.

Companies

You might also consider incorporating your business by forming a company. As a shareholder in a private company "limited by shares", your liability is limited, in most circumstances, to any unpaid share capital. This means that any assets you own personally cannot normally be used to pay off the company's debts, unless you have provided personal guarantees to a creditor (such as a bank) in respect of the company's liabilities.

One of the main benefits of setting up a business as a company, is the potential to plan and manage tax exposures. This applies particularly where trading profits are likely to be fairly significant, and/ or if you have family employed in the business.

Profits may be extracted from a trading company in a variety of ways including wages, dividends and employer pension contributions. If the company uses premises or other assets belonging to the shareholders, it might also be sensible for the company to pay a rent for same, subject to personal income tax and capital gains tax considerations. This will again depend on personal circumstances, but a key point about companies is the flexible tax planning opportunities they offer, relative to other business structures.

Of course, there are also some drawbacks to a company structure. It is likely to be more expensive to form and administer a company than a sole trader or partnership. The accounts, which must comply with the Companies Act, are held on the public record (albeit only limited information for small companies); there are stricter rules governing the running of the company and preparation of accounts; and there are some limited circumstances where the directors may still be held personally liable for the business's debts.

In summary, when it comes to choosing a business structure, there is no "one size fits all". How you choose to set-up should depend on careful consideration of issues including the level of profit you expect your business to make, your other earnings, your family's circumstances and the amount of financial risk you are prepared to accept.

For more on this subject visit www.scholesca.co.uk/blog/selecting-the-right-structure-for-your-start-up.

49

Paying yourself

If you are a sole trader or a partner in a partnership, paying yourself is a relatively simple matter. You simply draw from the business your share of the profits (and if you're a sole trader, that's 100% of the profits!).

If you're a sole trader, you may not even operate a separate business bank account. From a tax perspective, it really doesn't matter; whether or not you take money out of any business bank account or leave it in has no bearing at all on the profits the business will report, or the profits (or indeed losses) that end up in your income tax return.

If, on the other hand, you run a company, then you'll need to decide how you're going to pay yourself since, on the face of it, it's the company that's trading and making the profits – not you; remember

Paying yourself

that a company, unlike a sole trade or partnership, is regarded in law as a totally separate "legal being".

If you run a company, a number of things need to be borne in mind when deciding what to pay yourself, including:

- The corporation tax and national insurance (NIC) implications for the company;
- The income tax and NIC implications for yourself (and anyone else in the family who happens to be an employee and/ or shareholder);
- The amount of money you need to fund your lifestyle;
- The amount of money you want to set aside for retirement;
- The financial capacity of the business to pay you;
- whether you need to demonstrate a certain level of income for personal purposes (e.g. to secure a mortgage); and
- If you have lent money to the company, whether getting the loan repaid should take priority over getting a salary.

Clearly, paying yourself is not always *just* about extracting the maximum amount of money from the company at the lowest possible tax rate.

That said, if keeping the tax bills down *is* the primary objective, the way this is normally done is by i) taking a salary at the NIC "primary threshold" (£8,632 for the 2019/20 tax year) and ii) taking any further money as a dividend, provided there are sufficient distributable profits available.

There are several reasons why this approach is often adopted:

- There is no NIC payable by the employee or employer on a salary at this level, yet the employee should still receive a qualifying year's contribution for state pension purposes provided the salary is payrolled;

- The salary, being a cost of trading, will reduce the company's corporation tax bill;

- If the individual has no other taxable income, then the salary will fall within their income tax personal allowance, so there will be no income tax on the salary;

- Dividend income falling within the individual's basic rate income tax band will be taxed at the basic rate of income tax (currently 7.5%); and

- Dividends are not earnings so do not attract an NIC charge for the company or the individual.

If your company has *significant* profits available to distribute as dividends, the focus sometimes then switches to carefully managing the amount of dividends voted in any one income tax year. This is because the basic rate of income tax on dividends, 7.5%, steps up to 32.5% for higher rate payers and 38.1% (at the time of writing) for additional rate payers. That's a whole lot of tax, which is precisely

Paying yourself

why, if you run your own company, you need to make sure you understand the income tax consequences *before* voting a dividend!

What's more, those bright sparks over at HM Treasury have, in recent years, implemented various tax "cliff edges" for those with taxable incomes above £50,000 (the High Income Child Benefit Charge); £100,000 (the income tax personal allowance gets chopped at this level); and £150,000 (at which point they start restricting the amount you can put away in a pension without tax massive penalties).

So generally, the name of the game (at the time of writing), if you wish to avoid paying income tax at higher rates, is to keep your total taxable income (from salary, dividends, and any other sources) within about £50,000 each tax year. Of course, you *must* seek professional tax advice specific to your own circumstances before proceeding – for obvious reasons I can only offer a general overview here.

Finally, it would be remiss of me not to mention here the important role that employer pension contributions can play in extracting profits from companies in a very tax effective way. If your company has the cash available, consider whether it should make an employer pension contribution to your pension scheme.

Employer pension contributions, as a cost of trading, should save the company corporation tax. You won't pay tax on the contribution your scheme receives, as long as the contribution falls within the pension annual allowance (normally £40,000 per tax year, at the time of writing). And (hopefully) the money within your pension scheme will then be invested and grow, tax free, until you eventually retire – at which point you can start to draw it down. Again, professional advice is essential in this area.

50

Pricing and customers

Pricing decisions present a challenge for all business owners. In the search for greater profitability, should you raise or lower your prices - or just keep them the same? What would be the effect on profits of a significant price increase or reduction?

I can't offer a "one size fits all" answer within the scope of this chapter, but what I would like to do is highlight one or two important points about how the pricing decisions you make can have surprising consequences for the profitability of your business.

Let's look at a simple example now.

Selling at £20/ unit

Let's imagine a simple example. Let's say you sell a product for £20/ unit; it costs £10/ unit to make; and your overheads are £10,000. In year 1 you sell 1,100 units, so your profit & loss account looks like this:

- £22,000 sales   (1,100 units x £20/ unit)
- £11,000 costs of sale   (1,100 units x £10/ unit)
- £10,000 overheads
- £1,000 net profit

Selling at £22/ unit

Now, let's say that for year 2, you decide to *raise* prices by 10% to £22/ unit. By raising prices, however, you'll probably sell less units (some customers will buy from alternative suppliers, buy substitute products or perhaps just make do without). So let's say you sell only 950 units in year 2:

- £20,900 sales   (950 units x £22/ unit)
- £9,500 costs of sale   (950 units x £10/ unit)
- £10,000 overheads
- £1,400 net profit

Despite a 14% reduction in sales volumes of 150 units in year 2, the business has still *increased* profits by 40% to £1,400!

Selling at £18/ unit

Alternatively, let's imagine that for year 2, you decide instead to *reduce* prices by 10% to £18/ unit. By reducing prices, you'll presumably be hoping to sell lots more units! But how many more units would you actually need to sell to achieve the same net profit, £1,000, as in year 1?

The answer is 1,375 units, a massive 25% increase on the amount sold in year 1:

- £24,750 sales   (1,375 x £18/ unit)
- £13,750 costs of sale   (1,375 x £10/ unit)
- £10,000 overheads
- £1,000 net profit

How many units would you need to sell at £18/ unit to make the same amount of profit, £1,400, as if you'd raised the price to £22/ unit? The answer is 1,425 units, a huge 30% increase on the 1,100 units sold in year 1!

Will dropping the price to £18 result in a 30% increase in sales volumes? That could be *really* hard to achieve.

Comments

Effective pricing requires a sound understanding of profit margins and the relationship between profit margins, sales volumes, and profitability.

On the question of whether to raise or lower prices, each case needs to be decided on its own merits. Customer behaviour will vary depending on the product or service you're selling, and the markets in which you operate.

However, do think about *how else* you can differentiate your product or service from those of your competitors – price is not the only element in the "marketing mix". What can you do to compete and differentiate your business from the competition in terms of the product itself (quality or features); how you deliver or distribute it; and how you promote it? If you can compete on some or all these factors, you may be able to charge a premium price for your product or service.

Ultimately, it's hard to argue with the mathematical effects of pricing decisions, as illustrated in the simple examples above: raising prices when you are able to will normally do more to boost your business's profitability than *any other single action*.

51

Registering for VAT

VAT registration is usually mandatory where the value of taxable supplies made in the UK in the course of a business exceeds the VAT registration threshold in any twelve month period (unless the breach is due to exceptional circumstances); or where the value of taxable supplies is expected to exceed the registration threshold in the next thirty days alone. At the time of writing, the VAT registration threshold is £85,000.

A common misconception is that the twelve month test applies only to the turnover figure in the annual accounts of the business - not so! The twelve month test must be applied on a *rolling* twelve month basis, so unregistered traders who are in any danger of breaching the threshold need to perform the test *every month* - not just once a year.

Here are examples of how the basic tests apply in practice:

Twelve month test

Fred's accounts for the first twelve months of trading to 31st March 2019 showed taxable turnover for his clothing retail business of £80,000. At that point he was not yet VAT registered - and was not required to be because his taxable sales on a rolling twelve month basis had not exceeded the registration threshold of £85,000 at any time up to that point.

Continuing the pattern of growth in monthly sales, April 2019 turns out to be very busy with turnover of £12,000; his turnover for April 2018, by contrast, was only £5,000.

Therefore on a rolling twelve month basis, taxable turnover for the twelve months ended 30th April 2019 was £87,000, which exceeds the registration threshold of £85,000. Fred should apply for VAT registration by 30th May 2019 and he will become VAT registered effective from 1st June 2019.

Thirty day test

Sally's company is not VAT registered. On 1st April 2019 she realises that the company's taxable supplies in the next 30 days alone will exceed £85,000. Sally should apply for VAT registration no later than 30th April 2019 and the company will be registered from the date she realised the threshold would be exceeded, in this case 1st April 2019.

Other considerations

Failing to register for VAT on time is, unfortunately, a fairly common occurrence. Traders often misunderstand how the registration tests work; or fail to realise that penalties can apply if HMRC is not notified within specified timescales.

In the case of the rolling twelve month test, HMRC should be notified within thirty days of the end of the period in which the registration threshold is exceeded. In the case of the thirty day test, notification should take place within thirty days of when it is realised that the turnover will exceed the threshold in the next thirty days alone.

Where a business has gone over the registration threshold but wishes to avoid having to register, an exception may be sought from HMRC if it can be shown that the breach was due to one-off, exceptional circumstances. A request for an exception should be made within 30 days of having breached the threshold, and applicants are expected to be able to show that taxable turnover in the following 12 months will not breach the deregistration threshold, currently £83,000.

Businesses who are typically in a repayment position (i.e. those with zero-rated sales) and do not wish to register for VAT can apply to HMRC for an exemption from registration.

Traders may register for VAT voluntarily where taxable supplies do not exceed the threshold, as long as some level of taxable supplies is made, or intended to be made. Voluntary registration is common not only where the trader's taxable supplies are approaching the registration threshold, but also in many other circumstances.

Voluntary registration is often attractive to the start up business that expects to incur a lot of purchase VAT during the early days of operation.

Registering for VAT may also offer traders the prospect of recovering purchase VAT that has already been incurred on goods and services acquired for the purpose of the trade, subject to the detailed rules on "pre-registration VAT".

HMRC's VAT Notice 700/1 explains the registration requirements in further detail.

For more information about VAT registration, read my blog www.scholesca.co.uk/blog/vat-the-basics.

52

Employing staff

Employing staff is a big deal, no question about it. As well as the financial aspects, there are many legal aspects to consider.

I use the word "employing" in a broad sense – depending on how your business operates, you may have a choice between actually taking on employees, or using subcontractors instead, or even a combination. Let's compare the two options.

Subcontractors

Subcontractors (or freelancers) are not employees in the strict sense – they are self employed people who provide services to your business under contractual agreements (written or otherwise). Contracts for services, rather than a contract of service.

When you engage a subcontractor, your business does not normally assume any of the responsibilities associated with employing staff – so you don't have to give them annual leave or pay sick pay, and you don't have to operate payroll, deal with PAYE, pay employer's NIC or pension contributions, or give them notice. Neither do you need employer's liability insurance cover.

Using subcontractors can therefore offer more flexibility - useful if your labour requirements vary a lot from one period to the next.

On the other hand, unlike with employees, subcontractors may be free to walk away at short notice, which may create a problem when it leaves your business short of people to do the work that needs to be done. Subcontractors may also be more expensive than employees - even when all the additional costs of employing staff are factored in.

Employees

Taking on employees will normally be a necessity in the long run, if you are trying to build a substantial business and a team committed to achieving your vision.

Employees work under a contract of service (as opposed to a contract for services) and under UK employment law they must be provided with a written statement of terms within two weeks of joining your business.

The main benefits of taking on employees, rather than subcontractors, is that they are more likely to stay with you, may be more committed to the cause, and they may be cheaper than subcontractors, even when the additional costs of employment are taken into account.

On the other hand, when you employ staff, your business will have to operate a payroll (or outsource that work to an accountant), deal with PAYE, pay holiday pay, sick pay, employer's NIC, and employer's pension contributions under Auto Enrolment.

Employees have to be paid even when times are bad, and if you need to let them go, they will be entitled to notice which means you normally have to keep paying them, at least for a few weeks.

When you employ staff you will need employer's liability insurance, too.

There is also a whole raft of employment law to comply with where employees are concerned, including health & safety law. You'll need to establish HR policies and procedures to deal with things like grievances and complaints, discrimination, and all that nasty stuff.

Having a good HR adviser at the end of the phone is invaluable when it comes to staying the right side of employment law – especially when things don't work out with an employee.

Finally, if you employ staff, you need to adopt good performance management practices, including training & development and regular performance appraisals. You become responsible for their welfare in the workplace and their development and progression – so you'll want to invest in them and make sure your business provides an environment where they can flourish and contribute.

HMRC, employment status and IR35

Small business financial management

This one is a real hot potato. The topic of "employment status" is continually in the news. The question, from a tax perspective, is this — is a subcontractor really self employed — or are they *really* an employee?

It's important for you to understand the issue because the obligation to get the worker's status right often rests with the employer. If you treat an individual as a subcontractor and do not operate PAYE, but HMRC looks at how the relationship operates and decides that the relationship in fact amounts to one of employment, rather than self employment, then your business can end up being liable for the NIC and income tax it "should" have deducted.

The key test here is "mutuality of obligation" - though HMRC will look at all other aspects of the relationship between your business and the subcontractor, too. "Mutuality of obligation" simply means: does your business have to provide the subcontractor with work — and, when work is offered, does the subcontractor have to accept it?

If there is no "mutuality of obligation", it is less likely the subcontractor would be viewed by HMRC as an employee for PAYE purposes. If there is, it is highly likely they would be, though other factors have to be considered too before a definitive conclusion can be reached.

Also, if a subcontractor is working through their personal company, and you treat them as a self-employed subcontractor and do not operate payroll, but HMRC decides that — regardless of any paperwork there may be – the individual is *in reality* an employee, then they can invoke something known as "IR35".

When IR35 is applied, your subcontractor can end up paying income tax on their earnings with you – even though they are trading as a company. It all ends up getting messy and expensive. Further, from April 2020 the responsibility for assessing employment status for IR35 purposes will generally move from the subcontractors to the employer.

HMRC have an online employment status checking tool. If you are unsure about the employment status of someone you are taking on, HMRC claim that if you put the details into the status checker it will give you their assessment and that will be binding on HMRC, as long as the details have all been entered correctly.

However, the status checker is definitely not without criticism, as many claim that the answers it produces often do not agree with recent case law on the subject. If in doubt, take professional advice.

Tax aspects of employing staff

As an employer, your business needs to be registered with HMRC for PAYE. Payroll needs to be prepared whenever employees are paid, and electronic submissions made to HMRC. HMRC needs to be paid the income tax and NIC by the 22nd following the end of each "tax month" (tax months run 6th to 5th).

For a while now, employers have also had Auto Enrolment to deal with. Under Auto Enrolment, employers have to contribute to a pension for their employees, though some employers may be excluded from this requirement and employees can also "opt out" of the system. Auto Enrolment is generally dealt with as part of the payroll process, though there are additional requirements to comply with too, so take advice!

In addition to pensions, other aspects of payroll include sick pay, maternity/ paternity pay, holiday pay, student loan deductions, and other "wage arrestments". All in all it is a minefield and, unless you absolutely know what you are doing, most employers will find it more cost effective to outsource payroll to a good accountant, rather than attempting to deal with it all in-house.

Your employees need to be given a payslip every time they are paid, the payslips show their gross pay and deductions, and net pay. They also need to be given a P60 annually (which summarises their pay and deductions for the year), or a P45 if they leave during the tax year, and a P11D if they receive taxable benefits or expenses.

Payslips do not need to be in paper form any more – my firm Scholes CA provides electronic payslips instead, which are more efficient to distribute and better for the environment, too.

When budgeting to take on employees, remember that the true cost to your business will include not just their salary, but also employer's NIC (at 13.8% above the secondary threshold), pension contributions, and, potentially, the costs of recruiting them and training them.

53

Marketing

Marketing is essential if you want to grow your business. It costs money, so you need to make sure you're getting a return on your spend.

How much should you spend on marketing your products/ services? There are some important points to consider:

- What are your goals for the year ahead – in terms of revenue, profitability, new products or markets?
- What are conditions like in the market? Is there growing demand for your product?
- What's the competition like in your market?
- How much do you think you can afford to spend?

I'd like to be able to give you a "hard and fast" rule about how much you should budget to spend on marketing each year, but the truth is there is no such rule. Some people suggest that a budget around 5-10% of turnover is appropriate, but it really depends on your specific situation. Other methods include:

- Basing budgeted marketing spend on last year's spend, perhaps adjusted for inflation;

- Identifying the marketing activities the business wishes to do, pricing them up, and then "cutting the cloth" accordingly;

- A mixture of both of the above; and

- No fixed budget whatsoever, just a random approach.

If you want to be more scientific about budgeting for marketing activities, however, there are two things you need to figure out:

1. How much a customer is worth to your business; and

2. The average conversion rate from enquiry to customer.

Armed with this information, it may be possible to work out what you can afford to spend to attract new customers.

Let's say for example each extra customer generates on average £500 of gross profits over the lifetime of their relationship with your business. And your conversion rate is 1% - that is, for every 100 prospects you target, one becomes a customer. To get a return on your investment, you are looking at spending no more than £5.00

per prospect (that's 100 prospects x 1% conversion rate x £500 gross profits per new customer = £500 of profits generated from every 100 prospects). So in this example you don't want to spend more than £5.00 per prospect, because the cost would outweigh the expected returns.

Note two things here i) we are concerned with gross profit, not sales value and ii) we are thinking about the *total* value of all sales to that new customer – not just the first sale you make to them.

In the real world, it may be hard to establish these metrics with any certainty – though if your business has been up and running a while, you might have quite good data on which to base your assumptions.

Either way though, working through the above approach encourages discipline and focus on what an appropriate marketing budget is – and which types of campaign are more likely to generate a return, given that different campaigns will cost different amounts of money and realise different conversion rates.

When you are deciding which financial KPI's to establish and monitor, consider what metrics you can use to monitor how effective your marketing activities are. If you can you monitor your return on your marketing investment by tracking how many additional £'s of gross profit you generate for each £1 of marketing spend, this completes the circle.

If you are able to break this down even further by establishing the effectiveness of individual campaigns on sales through individual channels, even better, as this will help you refine and improve your marketing activities by building on what works and dropping the things that don't work.

54

Buying business premises

Buying business premises is a major decision. It often marks a significant milestone in the growth and development of a business, establishing a long-term base with an asset of significant value. There are of course also benefits to working from home, or leasing premises, so the decision needs to be weighed up carefully.

Benefits of working from home include the fact that you'll have no commute; lower overheads; and more flexible working hours.

The benefits of renting office space (compared to working from home) include the fact you might be less tempted to do work at home, which might be good for your work-life balance; also, your customers might expect you to have an office.

Leasing, rather than buying, business premises also provides more flexibility and requires less commitment (financial and emotional!)

than buying premises. The downside is that all that money ends up in someone else's pocket.

There are many factors that need to be considered when deciding whether to finally make the commitment and buy business premises, including:

- Is it the right option, or should the business continue to lease premises instead?
- Whether to buy it in your own name, your company's name, or perhaps another way (through your pension maybe)?
- How to finance the purchase, and on what terms?
- Tax considerations.

In whose name should the premises be bought? This is an interesting question. One shouldn't necessarily assume that business premises would always be bought by the business itself, as sometimes this may not be the best route. The determining factors will usually be i) how the purchase is to be financed and ii) what would be the most tax effective way to acquire and own the property?

For a business that is structured as a company, the three most common options are:

1. The company buys the property;
2. The business owner buys the property and rents it to the company;

3. The business owner's pension scheme (a SIPP or SSAS) buys the property and rents it to the company.

Let's examine each of those options in turn.

Option 1: company buying the premises

The company buying the property itself is perhaps the most straightforward of the three options. It raises the deposit, borrows the rest (normally on a bank term loan), the property goes on the balance sheet as a fixed asset, and the company repays the loan and interest over an agreed term.

The interest will usually be a tax-deductible trading expense (assuming the business occupies the building rather than, say, renting it out).

The lender will usually require that the property itself is put up as security for the loan, which means that in the event the company does not stick to the repayment schedule, the bank can take over the property.

Option 2: business owner buys the premises

Alternatively, the business owner could buy the property themselves and rent it to the company.

This used to be a really great wheeze but recent changes in CGT Entrepreneur's Relief have made it... not quite as good. But it's still an option to consider.

The rent paid by the company is normally a tax deductible trading expense for the company; in the business/ property owner's hands, the rent is of course income, so income tax will be payable on the profits from letting the premises to the business. Those profits will include the rental income less interest on any loan, and other general maintenance and running costs.

Buying business premises personally and renting them back to the company can be a *relatively* tax efficient way to take profits out of the company since, unlike with a salary, there is no NIC on property income.

Another important tax aspect to consider is chargeable gains. If the company bought the premises and subsequently disposed of it and made a gain (i.e. sold it for more than it originally cost to buy), the company would pay corporation tax on the gain. Nowadays there is no relief for any future gains attributed to inflation, incidentally. There would potentially then be further tax to pay, if the business owner then wanted to take the remaining sales proceeds out of the company.

If the business owner bought the premises themselves and subsequently sold it and made a gain, the individual would pay capital gains tax. Individuals enjoy a capital gains tax annual exempt amount (currently £12,000) but gains beyond this amount will be liable to capital gains tax (at rates of 10% or 20%, currently).

If the premises are sold as part of the disposal of the whole business, Entrepreneur's Relief may be available, and if that is the case then the rate of tax payable on any gain may be only 10% *however*

Entrepreneur's Relief is restricted where the property has been let by the individual to the company at a commercial rate. So be warned — there are disadvantages to renting your business property to your company too.

In the current climate banks will typically lend up to about 70% of the value of the property, so the other 30% you'll have to find.

Option 3: using a pension scheme

Using a pension scheme to buy business premises can be extremely tax effective.

It works as follows. The pension scheme buys the premises and rents it back to the company. The rent paid by the company is a tax deductible trading expense for the company, saving corporation tax.

The rent received by the pension scheme is not taxed at that point (since income and gains within registered pension schemes are not taxed). The rental income can be reinvested by the pension scheme to achieve further income and gains (hopefully!).

When the business owner retires, they can take their pension income, including the 25% tax free lump sum. It is likely the pension income the business owner takes in future will be taxed at lower rates of income tax than had they taken the income (as salary or rent) during the time they were working, since income in retirement tends to be lower than during the working phase of one's life.

The pension scheme does not necessarily sell the premises when the business owner retires or sells the business, incidentally — it could continue to own and rent the premises to a new commercial tenant.

Tax traps

There are several tax traps for the unwary when it comes to buying commercial premises. A discussion of these is really beyond the scope of this book, but I will mention a couple of points briefly.

Stamp Duty Land Tax (in Scotland, Land & Buildings Transaction Tax; in Wales, Land Transaction Tax) is normally payable when business premises are acquired. It is based on set percentages of the amount payable for the premises and the percentages step up as the price of the property goes up. So you need to factor the cost of these taxes into your budget. These taxes are also payable on some lease premiums, as well as outright purchases, incidentally.

One more thing: you have to pay VAT when you buy "new" commercial property or property that the vendor has "opted to tax" (more of that in a minute). Stamp duty is calculated based on the total price, *including* any VAT you have to pay on the property. Ouch!

It is relatively uncommon to have to pay VAT when you buy business premises, but there are two circumstances where you might have to:

1. If the commercial premises are "new" (less than three years old);
2. Where the seller has "opted to tax" the property.

If VAT is chargeable, you should not assume that the VAT your business pays can be recovered from HMRC. This will depend on who is buying the property, how the property will be used, and in some circumstances, whether the buyer in turn "opts to tax" the property. You *must* get proper advice from your lawyer and accountant when considering any property transaction. VAT should *always* be at the forefront of your thinking when it comes to property matters.

55

Raising finance

When your business needs to raise money, it's important to understand the types of finance able, and to be able to identify which types are appropriate for the situation.

Essentially there are three types of finance we may be concerned with: equity finance; debt finance (in other words borrowing); and grants.

With equity finance, the person providing the money gets a stake in the business – which may be on the same terms as existing investors, or on different terms – it depends on the specific situation.

With debt finance, the lender does not get a stake in the business, instead they get the right to be repaid, normally with interest added, over an agreed period of time.

Grant finance is a bit like debt finance but you don't have to pay the money back provided the conditions of the grant are met.

Let's compare the advantages of debt and equity finance.

Advantages of debt compared to equity

- The lender does not get a stake in the business, so the existing investors' stake in the business is not diluted;
- The lender does not get to participate in the profits of the business – so they don't get any extra benefit when the business grows and profits increase;
- The interest charged on the debt is normally deductible against the business's trading profits for tax purposes;
- The costs of repaying the debt and interest are usually known (except where the interest is at a variable rate), which means the business can plan for those costs with reasonable certainty; and
- Compared to raising equity, obtaining debt is usually more straightforward, less heavily regulated and requires less administration.

Advantages of equity compared to debt

- Except with redeemable or preference shares, there is usually no automatic obligation to pay investors a dividend or buy their shares back;

- Too much debt can cause problems for a business if it is unable to cover the cost of the interest and meet the repayment schedule, so equity is sometimes a better alternative if the business already has a lot of debt (if it is already "highly geared");

- A highly geared company may be perceived by lenders/investors as a risky bet, so equity investment may be preferred to adding further debt in some cases;

- Businesses (or their owners) often have to put up assets as security for debt, including personal guarantees, but this is not the case with equity, so if the business or its owners are unwilling or unable to put up assets as security, then equity may be a better route;

- Loans often come with restrictive covenants – basically legally binding agreements that require the business to manage their financial affairs within strictly defined boundaries, until the loan is repaid. Stepping outside those boundaries can result in the business being required to repay the loans immediately, which can be fatal if the business does not have the necessary funds or is unable to refinance. Equity finance, by contrast, usually comes with no such conditions;

- Debt providers will usually play no role in helping you manage or grow the business; equity holders, by contrast, may sit on the board and may bring valuable expertise to the table.

Angel investment

Angel investment can be a good option for companies looking to raise capital during the early stages of life. Investments typically range from £10k to £500k and you will get one (or more) partners on board who will hopefully bring deep experience and great contacts to bear, to help you grow the business. A disadvantage is that angel investment is normally made as equity, so your interest in the company is likely to be diluted at least to some degree - but that's the quid pro quo for getting an experienced angel on board.

Raising equity finance is a complex area with many legal, as well as financial considerations. Offering shares in a private limited company to members of the public is an activity regulated in the UK by the Financial Conduct Authority so specialist advice must be sought if you are thinking of heading down this avenue.

For the remainder of this chapter we will focus on debt and grant finance, as these are, far and away, the more significant types of finance used by small businesses.

Types of debt finance

There are probably as many types of debt finance as there are flavours of ice cream, so we'll focus on a few of the most common categories:

- Directors' loans;
- Friends & family;
- Bank borrowing;
- Asset finance;
- Invoice finance;
- Merchant cash advances;
- Credit cards;
- Fixed income (bonds); and
- Peer to peer.

Key considerations

Debt finance usually comes at a cost, so the name of the game, usually, is to find the cheapest option and to avoid, as far as possible, having to put up any assets as security.

You'll also want to match the maturity of the debt you are seeking with the thing you want to finance. Short term debt (like a bank overdraft) should not be used to fund long term needs – and vice-versa.

Businesses will often use a mixture of short-term and long-term debt, reflecting the purpose to which the money is put, and you need to get the mix right.

Directors' loans

In a small company, the directors (who are often also the main or only shareholders) frequently provide finance in the form of loans. These loans may be interest free or interest bearing (the latter has important tax consequences for both the company and the individual), secured or unsecured, and may be subject to a formal loan agreement or, very frequently, made on informal terms with no fixed repayment schedule.

It is important to appreciate that an unsecured director's loan to the company is at risk – in the event the company goes under, the director is in the same position as most other creditors, so think carefully before lending money to your business on unsecured terms.

Friends and family

Friends and family may be persuaded to lend money to your business. If you're running a start up, they may be the first port of all - especially if banks are not yet quite ready to take an interest!

Mostly, loans from friends and family will be a low cost, relatively low risk option – since they are your friends and family, presumably (!) they will be prepared to help you out, which likely means no (or low) interest and, probably, no expectation of security.

Bank overdrafts

Bank overdrafts may be suitable to fund a business's working capital requirements, although they don't come cheap (which is why you want to manage your working capital effectively, as you'll recall from earlier!).

They may be secured against the business's assets, and/ or with a personal guarantee from the owners, or unsecured – it depends on the business and what the bank is willing to offer. Everyone knows how a bank overdraft works, so I won't explain further.

Bank term loans

Term loans may be a suitable option to finance a long-term plan, such as buying business premises. They will normally be secured and subject to a predetermined repayment schedule; the interest rate may be fixed or variable.

Asset finance

Finance leases and hire-purchase agreements are often used to finance the acquisition of fixed assets (like plant & machinery or vehicles). The debt under the agreement is secured against the asset itself and normally the payments are due over a relatively short term – typically between three and five years. Asset finance is a popular way for businesses to acquire the kind of assets that depreciate relatively quickly.

Operating leases, by contrast, are used to *hire* assets for a specified period, but ownership reverts to the lessor at the end of the term. There are also hybrid arrangements that give businesses the option (but not the obligation) to buy the asset at the end of the lease term.

Invoice finance

There is a variety of invoice finance options (invoice discounting, factoring) that can help businesses fund cash flow. These are effectively secured against the company's trade debtors. Invoice financing can be a very expensive way to fund working capital, so other options should generally be exhausted first.

Merchant cash advances

Merchant cash advances are unsecured advances of cash based on future debit/ credit card sales. They are repaid based on an agreed percentage of the business's card sales transactions. If the cash advance takes longer to pay off, the agreed repayment cost remains the same.

Credit cards

Company credit cards can be useful for managing and keeping track of purchases made by employees – particularly those who travel away and need to pay travel and subsistence costs locally – but the balance should be paid off *every month* if at all possible because the interest costs can be very expensive.

Fixed income (bonds)

Companies sometimes issue bonds to investors to finance long-term plans. Bonds are basically long-term debts with a fixed rate of interest, and may be redeemed at a specified future point, the "maturity date". Interest is usually payable at fixed intervals. Important tax considerations apply, so seek advice from your accountant.

Peer to peer

There is a variety of "alternative finance" options available these days, with peer to peer being perhaps the best known. Platforms such as Funding Circle provide a way for businesses to obtain funding from other businesses or individuals on agreed terms. If your bank is unable or unwilling to help, the peer to peer network may provide a suitable alternative, though you will need to check and compare the terms on offer as peer to peer loans can be relatively expensive.

Grant funding

Grant funding may be available to support your business's plans. Grants may be available for a variety of purposes, funding capital expenditure and/ or revenue costs. Your local enterprise agency will usually be the place to start.

Some grants are paid with no conditions attached; if your business meets the criteria and gets the grant, it is then free to proceed as it wishes.

Other grants can come with very strict terms and conditions attached, and if the business fails to meet those conditions, the grant (or a portion of the grant) may be required to be repaid. In that sense, a grant can be a bit like a loan – so be careful to stick to the terms and conditions of any grants your business receives.

56

The impact of taxation

This is not a book about taxation, a subject which would merit not just one book but probably a dozen! Nevertheless, as a small business owner it is *crucial* that you arm yourself with *some* knowledge of taxation, if only at a rudimentary level, because just about every financial transaction your business undertakes and every financial decision you make will have a tax implication of one kind or another (and often, more than one!).

As the UK tax code is so complex and massive, *the most important thing of all* is to seek professional advice any time you are planning for your business to do anything that is outwith its "normal" activities - by which I mean anything that it has not already been doing for some time. May I give you a few examples?

- Any transactions involving land / buildings;

- Buying, leasing, selling or renting any other significant assets;
- Undertaking research & development activities;
- Creating, buying or selling intellectual property (e.g. patents);
- Hiring or firing staff;
- Starting to trade or ceasing to trade;
- Selling the business;
- Starting to trade in a new jurisdiction;
- Changing the nature of the business's activities (for example new products or new ways of operating),
- Starting a new trade alongside existing ones;
- Starting investment (as opposed to trading) activities, for example by renting out property to third parties;
- Significantly good, or bad, trading conditions/ financial results;
- A change in ownership of the business;
- Significant changes in the way the owners reward themselves.

All of the above may have significant tax implications for the business (often its owners too) and I really cannot emphasise enough the importance of getting professional advice in any of those circumstances.

And not only that, but also, getting advice *promptly* – where possible *before* the thing happens – is usually the way to go. The reason for this is simple: good advice received before you do something may lead you to make a different – hopefully better – decision, in terms of what you do and/ or when you do it.

Tax law works on the basis of facts – what did happen – rather than what everyone *wished* had happened in retrospect, so the time to get advice, wherever possible, is before the thing happens. For that simple reason, as a business owner tax should always - *always* - be at the forefront of your mind.

You want to anticipate what is going to happen, find out about the tax effects, and assess the tax effects of any alternative courses of action so that you can make the best decision in the circumstances.

See that motorhome your company was going to buy because you travel away a lot? That's probably a car for taxable benefit in kind purposes.

That property you're about to buy? The vendor has "opted to tax" it, so you'll probably have to pay VAT, and the Stamp Duty Land Tax you pay will be based on the total price – including the VAT. Don't assume you'll be able to recover the VAT because that isn't a given, either!

That new piece of equipment you were going to acquire under a finance lease – have you thought about the tax cash flow advantages of using hire purchase instead?

That employee you're about to take on – have you registered for PAYE? Have you budgeted for the NIC and the pension contributions you'll probably need to be making? I could go on, but hopefully you've got the idea...

Changes in tax rules may also affect the business, though a good accountant will help you keep in touch with significant changes and be able to advise you what you need to do in those circumstances.

So, what about the basics, then?

Corporation tax

If your business trades as a company (rather than as a sole trade or partnership) then it will be liable to pay corporation tax on the profits and any gains that it makes.

Profits and gains are worked out using tax rules rather than accounting rules, so the taxable profit for corporation tax purposes is rarely the same figure that appears in the profit & loss account. Though the numbers are sometimes very similar, they are rarely exactly the same. This is one of the things that people really struggle to get their heads around.

To work out the taxable profits for corporation tax purposes, accountants start with the profit figure shown in the accounts, but then they have to adjust it for various matters, including:

- To add back expenses that appear in the accounts but are not deductible for tax purposes (for example, depreciation charges, or most business entertainment);
- To deduct any income appearing in the accounts that is not taxable; and
- To claim "capital allowances" (that's relief that a business gets for the cost of "qualifying plant & machinery" - instead of getting relief for depreciation).

In a great many cases, the main reason why the company's taxable profit figure is different from the profit shown in the accounts is because of "capital allowances". The taxman does not give relief for most depreciation shown in accounts (the depreciation on assets under finance leases is one exception), instead there is a system of relief known as the capital allowances system which allows companies to claim deductions for the cost of acquiring plant & machinery.

The system is quite generous for smaller amounts of capital expenditure as these can generally be written off for tax purposes all in one go, even though they may be depreciated in the accounts over several years.

The current rate of corporation tax is 19% and it is set to reduce to only 17% from April 2020, which compares very favourably with UK income tax rates - especially if you are a Scottish taxpayer.

Corporation tax is usually payable nine months and one day after the end of the accounting period, and a corporation tax return must be submitted to HMRC within twelve months of the end of the period of account. Penalties apply for late payment or late submission of the return.

Income tax and NIC

If you trade as a sole trader or partnership, you will be liable to pay income tax and NIC on your income (or your share of the income if you are in partnership).

Unlike with corporation tax, with income tax the liability to pay the tax rests with you – not the business. So your profits (or indeed any losses) should be reported through the Self Assessment system, under which you have to file a tax return showing the income and gains you made (or were deemed to make) in each tax year.

If your sole trade/ partnership draws up accounts to some date other than the end of the tax year (say 30th June or 31st December, for example), then there are also rules about which tax year each year's profits are to be reported in, known as "basis period rules". This can get very technical, especially during the first few and last few years of the business, so you need to get advice from a good accountant about your specific circumstances.

For a business that has already been up and running for some time, though, the rule is that the taxable profits for a specific income tax year are based upon the accounts for the financial year that ended in the income tax year. So for example, a sole trader who draws up accounts to 31st December each year, will determine her taxable trading profits (or losses) for the tax year 6th April 2018 to 5th April

2019, with reference to her accounts for the year ended 31st December 2018.

Taxable trading profits for income tax purposes are calculated *broadly* in the same way as for corporation tax purposes.

In the UK, income tax years run from 6th April to 5th April, and Self Assessment returns have to be filed and any outstanding tax and NIC paid by 31st January immediately following the end of the tax year. Failure to comply leads to penalties and interest being charged on any late payment.

If you have been filing Self Assessment returns for some time, you may already be making "payments on account" on 31st January and 31st July annually.

PAYE and payroll

See the chapter "Employing staff".

VAT

See the chapter "Registering for VAT".

Capital Gains Tax

Capital gains tax (CGT) is paid by individuals through the Self Assessment system on gains they make on the sale or gifting of assets. In a business context, CGT can apply where an individual realises a gain on the sale or gift of a business asset. This could include, for example, the sale of business premises occupied by the business or let out to third parties; or the sale or gift of shares in a company.

The rates of CGT paid by individuals depend on what other taxable income they have in the tax year in which the gain arises. Gains falling within the basic rate are taxed at a lower rate (currently 10%), those falling within the higher rate band at a higher rate (currently 20%), though there is an additional surcharge for gains relating to the sale of residential property.

Individuals enjoy a CGT tax-free allowance each tax year known as the "annual exempt amount"; chargeable gains falling within the annual exempt amount are not taxed. Any unused amount is *not* carried forward.

CGT on most disposals is payable on 31st January immediately following the tax year in which the disposal took place. From April 2020 the payment due date for CGT on disposals of residential property is going to be accelerated so that payment will be due within 30 days of the disposal.

Various exemptions and reliefs exist that may reduce or even eliminate any CGT liability in some circumstances, particularly in relation to assets that are used in a business for trading purposes (typically not assets that are used for investment purposes). The principle CGT reliefs, in a business context, include:

- Rollover relief – where the proceeds from the sale of certain business assets are reinvested into certain other business assets within a specified timeframe, the gain arising on the sale may be deferred for a certain period of time, in some circumstances until the replacement asset is sold;

- Incorporation relief – where an existing business is incorporated (put into a company) in exchange for shares, the gains arising on the disposal of assets into the company may be deferred;

- Gift relief – where business assets (including shares in a trading company) are gifted (or sold at less than their market value), any gains arising may be deferred – the gains basically transfer to the recipient of the gift; and

- Entrepreneur's relief – when a business or a part of a business (including shares in a trading company) is sold, the taxpayer may qualify to pay CGT at a reduced rate of only 10% in some circumstances. The relief can extend to assets owned personally by the taxpayer, but used by the partnership business or company that is being sold – the typical example here is business premises owned by the taxpayer but used by the company, though restrictions apply where the company has paid a rent to occupy the premises, as discussed earlier.

The key point here is that, because asset disposals can usually be anticipated, there is usually an opportunity to take professional advice before the transaction takes place about the possible CGT consequences of the proposed transaction. A good accountant should be able to advise you of the CGT consequences, and about the existence of any CGT exemptions and reliefs that may be available, subject to meeting the correct conditions, to alleviate the tax burden.

Land Transaction Taxes

See the chapter "Buying business premises".

57

Selling up

If you want to maximise your financial return when you eventually sell your business, it can really pay to start organising and planning years, rather than months, beforehand.

Small business owners often don't realise as much on exit as they might, and for a number of reasons including:

- Over-dependence of the business on the exiting owner;
- Inefficient operations that lead to waste and profit leakage; and
- A failure to fully exploit available growth and profit opportunities.

The good news – especially if a sale is still a few years, rather than months away - is that there are many steps the small business owner can take to improve their chances of a profitable exit.

Focusing on improving profitability and reducing waste is important. A series of consistently strong (and improving) financial results will help to demonstrate to potential buyers the profitability and potential of the business. Small business owners are often strongly motivated to minimise tax liabilities by suppressing profits; but this can be counterproductive when it comes to being able to demonstrate the quality of the business to potential buyers! Focus on profitable growth, cutting out unprofitable activities and eliminating waste.

Reducing the business's reliance on the owner is often critical. Many small businesses are reliant - even totally dependent - on the proprietor to operate successfully. This presents a significant problem for a potential buyer. Build a strong management team and progressively transfer knowledge and skills to them. Consider how best to manage business-customer relationships so the goodwill is attached to the business and the brand, rather than to you as the current owner.

Maintaining accurate business records, including procedural and financial records, matters. We've already discussed all that! Comprehensive and accurate record keeping helps demonstrate to potential suitors the quality and robustness of the business, governance approach and underlying systems, procedures and internal controls.

You'll also need to deal with any major problems in the business wherever practicable; a potential buyer will seek to mark the price down for unresolved issues so consider if there are problems that need to be addressed now.

What can you do to improve the quality of your business's revenue streams? Buyers dislike uncertainty, particularly when it comes to the future earnings potential of the business. Consider whether income streams can be made more predictable, more regular, more long-term, and less concentrated on a few big customers. Examine your contractual arrangements with customers to see where improvements can be made.

Is your business's brand and intellectual property properly protected? For example, are there registrable trademarks, or processes/ products that can be patented, in order to protect the value in the business?

My final tip on preparing your business for sale: pay down debt. Reducing debt levels can help strengthen the balance sheet and reduce financial risk for a buyer. If the business has surplus cash, paying down debt, especially where the interest cost far exceeds any income earned on the cash, may make a lot of sense.

Depending on the specifics of your business, there might be a variety of other actions to consider too.

58

Choosing an accountant

If you are starting or already running a business, sooner or later you'll need to appoint an accountant if you don't already have one. But how do you choose who to go with?

The truth is, there is a vast difference between individual firms of accountants. From the exterior they can all look pretty similar, but when you get down to the nuts and bolts, every firm has its own culture, its own ways of doing things, different areas of expertise, different attitudes to using technology, different focus in terms of the types of clients it works with, different pricing.

So, how to choose an accountant? It's a complicated question. As human beings we're capable of making some really interesting choices. Countless studies have shown that we rarely make decisions for sound, rational reasons. Our limbic system makes sure we make decisions for all kinds of odd reasons - we just rationalise them after the event to make it seem like we know what we're doing!

So I'm not going to offer any magic pathways or psychological workarounds; instead I'm going to offer my take on some of the things you really should consider before picking an accountant. What you do with this information ultimately is up to you. At the very least, you can make it seem like you thought it through!

Values

Top of the list in my opinion - never mind all the stuff about cloud technology or clever tax schemes or what have you - is values. It's fair to say that as a profession we do kind of share a set of common values - trust, integrity, quality, confidentiality for example. So that doesn't really help you differentiate.

What I mean is: what does the firm stand for? What do the partners stand for? Does this resonate with you? Can they demonstrate how they live their values?

If you are an entrepreneurial, risk-taking, go-ahead type business, with plans to buy and expand, does the firm down the road share your interests and outlook?

If you are cautious and risk averse, is a sophisticated tax planning firm really right for you?

If you run a social enterprise, does the firm you're talking to have an interest in corporate social responsibility? Do they support local concerns?

Before anything else, and I mean anything else, question whether you share the same values. If you don't, sooner or later the wheels may come off.

Closely tied to this is...

People

Ultimately, and despite what the cloud accounting exponents will have you believe, at heart we are still a people business. Relationships matter. People matter. So it's important that you can form great professional relationships with your accountancy firm, founded on trust and mutual respect.

If you're checking out different accountants - running a "beauty parade", so to speak - do spend some time with the individuals who you'd be working with most, to get a feel for what they would be like to work with day to day. Get your staff involved too. You'll soon know if it's going to work or not.

Skills

Can the firm do what you need them to do? Top tip - never assume all accountants can do the same things. We all know that doctors can specialise in different areas of medicine. Accountants are no different. True, many smaller firms offer a similar range of services. But an increasing number specialise in specific areas or industries.

Make a list of the things you think you'll need the accountant to help with. Include the stuff you don't need now, that you might in a few years (unless perhaps you like changing your accountant regularly!). Ask them if they can do these things for you, and how they would go about it. You could even ask them for testimonies from other customers who work in the same industry as you.

Location

The least important of my "big four", your accountant's location is of some importance - but it probably shouldn't be a deal breaker. Technology has actually made it easier to work with your accountant of choice, even if they are based several hundred miles away.

At my firm Scholes CA (www.scholesca.co.uk) we have clients who are based *all over the country*, right down to the south coast of England, even though our offices are in Edinburgh – and Orkney!

In truth, despite advances in technology many small business owners still prefer to be able to see their accountant face to face. And that's OK. But don't discount a good suitor, just because they're not based just down the road. It really isn't hard to fix up a meeting if you really, really need one, and most routine stuff really can be done with your accountant over the internet these days.

Glossary

Accounting policies	The principles and practices applied by an entity to prepare its accounts
Accrual basis	Showing the effects of transactions and events based on when the occur, not when cash is received or paid
Amortisation	The allocation of the depreciable amount of an asset over its useful life – usually intangible assets
Asset	A resource controlled by the business that is expected to generate economic benefits in future
Associate	An entity over which the business has significant influence, that is neither a subsidiary nor a joint venture

Borrowing costs	Interest and other costs incurred by the entity in connection with borrowing funds
Carrying amount	The amount at which an asset or liability is shown in the accounts
Cash	Cash on hand
Cash equivalents	Short term, highly liquid investments that are easily converted into cash and which are unlikely to change in value
Cash flows	Inflows and outflows of cash and cash equivalents
Consolidated financial statements	The accounts of a parent and its subsidiaries presented as those of a single entity
Construction contract	A contract specifically for the construction of an asset or closely related group of assets
Constructive obligation	An obligation to another party (or parties) resulting from an entity's actions
Contingent asset	A possible asset arising from past events
Control	The power to govern the financial and operating policies of another entity so as to benefit from its activities

Credit risk	The risk that one party to a contract will not discharge its obligations, resulting in financial loss
Current assets	Assets of an entity that are not fixed assets
Current liabilities	Liabilities of an entity that, generally speaking, are required to be settled within twelve months of the date the balance sheet is made up to
Current tax	The amount of taxable payable or refundable for the current reporting period
Deferred income	Income invoiced/ money received in one financial period that is to be shown as income in a future reporting period (usually because it has not yet been earned)
Deferred tax	Tax recoverable or payable in future periods in respect of the future tax consequences of taxable profits/ losses reported
Deferred tax asset	Tax recoverable in future periods in respect of the future tax consequences of transactions and events recognised in the accounts
Deferred tax liability	Tax payable in future periods in respect of the future tax consequences of transactions and events recognised in the accounts

Defined benefit pension scheme	Pension schemes other than defined benefit schemes
Depreciable amount	The cost of an asset as shown in the accounts, less its estimated residual value
Depreciation	The allocation of the depreciable amount of an asset over its useful life – usually tangible assets
Effective interest method	A method of recognising the cost of a financial asset or liability (e.g. an interest bearing loan) over an appropriate period of time
Equity	The shareholders' interest in a company – the assets less the liabilities
Expenses	Outflows or depletions of assets and incurrences of liabilities that result in decreases in equity – apart from distributions to investors ("dividends")
Fair value	The amount for which an asset could be sold or liability exchanged between willing parties in an arm's length transaction
Finance lease	A lease that transfers to the lessee most of the risks and rewards associated with owning the asset (even if actual ownership does not or may not transfer)

Financial asset	Any asset that is: - Cash; - An equity instrument (e.g. shares in another company); or - A contractual right to receive cash or exchange financial assets or financial liabilities with another entity on potentially favourable terms Also some contracts that will or may be settled by the entity using equity instruments
Financial instrument	A contract that gives rise to a financial asset of one entity and a financial liability or equity instrument of another
Financial liability	Any liability that is a contractual obligation - To deliver cash or another financial asset; or - To exchange financial assets or financial liabilities with another entity on potentially unfavourable terms

	Also some contracts that will or may be settled by the entity using equity instruments
Financial position	The relationship of the assets, liabilities and equity of the business as reported in the balance sheet
Financial statements	The accounts, showing the financial performance, position, and cash flows of the business
Financing activities	Activities that result in a change in the business's equity or borrowings
Fixed assets	Assets of a business that are intended to be used on a continuing basis
FRS 102	The Financial Reporting Standard applicable in the UK and Republic of Ireland – the main financial reporting standard applied by small businesses
FRS 105	The Financial Reporting Standard applicable to the Micro-entities Regime – a financial reporting standard for very small businesses
Gains	Increases in economic benefits that are income but not revenue

Going concern	An entity is a going concern unless management intends to liquidate it or has no realistic alternative but to do so
Goodwill	Future economic benefits arising from assets that are not capable of being individually identified and separately recognised
Government grant	Financial assistance in the form of a transfer of resources (normally cash) in return for past or future compliance with specified conditions
Group	A parent and its subsidiaries
Impairment loss	The amount by which the carrying amount of an asset exceeds: • In the case of stock, its selling price less costs to complete; and • In other cases, its recoverable amount
Income	Increases in economic benefits in the form of inflows or enhancements of assets or decreases in liabilities that result in increases in equity – other than those resulting from contributions from equity investors

Income statement	The profit & loss account
Intangible asset	An identifiable non-monetary asset without physical substance. To be identifiable it must be: • Separable (capable of being sold, licensed, rented, exchanged etc); and • Arising from contractual or other legal rights
Inventory	Assets: • Held for sale; • In the process of being made for sale; or • In the form of materials or supplies to be consumed during the production of goods or rendering of services
Investing activities	The acquisition and sale of long-term assets and other investments not included in cash equivalents

Investment property	Property held by the owner (or lessee under a finance lease) to earn rental income or for capital appreciation, or both – rather than for productive or administrative purposes, or for sale in the ordinary course of business
Lease	An agreement whereby a lessor grants the right for another party (the lessee) to use an agreed asset for a period of time, in return for payment
Liability	An obligation arising from past events that is expected to result in an outflow of resources
Materiality	Errors and omissions in accounts are considered material if, individually or collectively, they would influence the economic decisions of users of those accounts
Non-current assets	Assets which an entity: • Does not expect to sell or consume in its normal trading cycle; • Does not hold primarily for trading purposes; or • Does not expect to sell in the 12 months after the balance sheet date

	Also cash and cash equivalents restricted from being exchanged or used to settle a liability in the 12 months after the balance sheet date
Notes (to the accounts)	Notes provide additional information about the business's financial performance and position, using narrative, disaggregations of items presented in the accounts, and information about matters not recognised in the accounts
Operating activities	The main revenue-producing activities of a business (not investing or financing activities)
Operating lease	A lease that does not transfer substantially all the risks and rewards of ownership to the lessee; a lease that is not an operating lease is a finance lease
Ordinary share	An equity instrument that is subordinate to all other classes of equity instrument
Other comprehensive income	Items of income and expense that are not recognised in the profit & loss account
Owners	Owners of equity instruments
Parent	An entity that has one or more subsidiaries

Performance	The relationship of income and expenses of an entity, as reported in the profit & loss account or statement of comprehensive income
Profit or loss	The total of income less expenses, excluding items classified as other comprehensive income
Property, plant & equipment	Tangible assets that: • Are held for use in the production or supply of goods or services, for rental to others, or for administrative purposes; and • Are expected to be used in more than one financial period
Provision	A liability of uncertain timing or amount; may be shown separately as a liability, or credited against related assets (e.g. fixed assets, stock, or debtors)
Recognition	The process of including in the accounts assets, liabilities, income and expenses where the following criteria are met: • It is probable that any future economic benefit associated with

	the item will flow to or from the entity; and • The value of the item can be measured reliably
Reconcile	The act of comparing a balance as stated in a business's financial records (such as a bank balance or an amount owed to a supplier) with a balance as stated on a document prepared by a third party (such as a bank statement or supplier statement of account), and identifying, investigating and resolving any differences between the two
Reconciliation	A document demonstrating how a balance in a business's accounting records compares with the balance stated on a third party document, setting out the reasons for any differences between the two (typically the only acceptable reason for a difference is where a transaction has been recorded in different reporting periods by each entity)
Recoverable amount	The higher of an assets fair value less costs to sell; or its value in use
Related party	A person or entity that is closely related to the entity that is preparing accounts – for

	example, close family members of the owners; other companies in the same group
Related party transaction	A transaction between the reporting entity and a related party
Reporting date/ balance sheet date	The end of the latest financial period covered by the accounts
Reporting period	The period covered by the accounts
Residual value (of an asset)	The estimated amount that an entity would realise (net of disposal costs) on the disposal of an asset, if that asset was currently in the condition it is expected to be in at the end of its useful life
Revenue	The gross inflow of economic benefits during a period arising from an entity's normal activities, other than increases relating to contributions from shareholders - otherwise known as "turnover" or "sales"
Statement of cash flows	The financial statement that provides information about changes in cash and cash equivalents in the period, showing separately changes arising from operating, investing and financing activities

Statement of comprehensive income	The financial statement that combines the income and expenses shown in the profit & loss account with other comprehensive income – the two are often combined into a single statement of comprehensive income
Statement of financial position	The financial statement that shows an entity's assets, liabilities and equity – otherwise known as a balance sheet
Subsidiary	An entity that is controlled by another entity
Taxable profit (or loss)	The profit (or loss) for a reporting period upon which corporation tax/ income tax is calculated
Turnover	The amounts derived from the sale of goods and services, after deduction of sales discounts, VAT and similar taxes
Useful life	The period over which an asset is expected to be available for use

Index

A

accountant
  choosing, 288
accounting concepts, 107
  assets, 108
  capital employed, 109
  equity, 108
  fundamental rule, 109
  liabilities, 108
  liquidity, 109
  solvency, 109
accounting controls, 91
accounting policies, 145
accounting software, 85
  and bank reconciliations, 49
  and banking, 48
  and budgeting, 163
  and cash flow forecasting, 159
  and payroll, 40
  and purchases, 25
  and sales, 20
  and the nominal ledger, 70
  and VAT returns, 54
  changing to new software, 88
accounts production process, 79
administration, 83
  delegating authority, 84
  record keeping requirements, 83
administrative expenses, 131
aged creditors
  and common problems with management accounts, 187
  and the nominal ledger, 77
  and the purchases process, 30
aged debtors
  and KPI's, 190
  and the nominal ledger, 77
  and the sales process, 21
assets

definition, 115
authorisation controls, 91

B

backing up accounting records, 78
balance sheet, 111
   and pre year end planning, 215
   assets - liabilities = equity, 123
   debits and credits, 73
   definition, 99
   example - business balance sheet, 114
   example - personal balance sheet, 112
   reviewing, 177
   strengthening, 220
bank accounts
   opening, 46
bank reconciliation, 48
   and the nominal ledger, 77
banking processes, 46
budgeting & forecasting, 160
   breakeven sales, 175
   processes, 81
   scenario testing, 163
   software, 168
   template, 162
business premises, 259
   buying, leasing or working from home, 259
   tax traps, 264
   who should buy?, 260
business structures, 231
   limited company, 234
   partnership, 232
   sole trader, 232

C

capital gains tax, 281
cash flow
   crisis management, 210
   HMRC time to pay arrangements, 212
   improvement of, 158
cash flow forecast, 155
   preparation, 157
   template, 156
cash flow statement, 139
   cash flow from financing activities, 141
   cash flow from investing activities, 141
   cash flow from operating activities, 141
   definition, 100
   direct method of preparation, 144
   example, 139
   indirect method of preparation, 144
   preparing and interpreting, 143
cash sales, 16
categorising expenditure, 26
   common problems with management accounts, 184
chart of accounts, 71
cloud software
   advantages, 86

vs desktop software, 86
comparability
    of financial statements, 149
completeness
    of financial statements, 149
construction industry scheme, 43
contribution margin, 176
corporation tax
    and pre year end planning, 214
    and tax compliance, 55
    calculation of taxable profits, 278
    in the profit & loss account, 134
    inclusion in budgets, 166
    inclusion in cash flow forecasts, 158
    payment and return due dates, 56
    rates, 279
cost of sales, 131
credit sales, 17
current assets
    definition, 117
current liabilities
    definition, 118
cut off
    and common problems with management accounts, 185

D

debits and credits, 73
depreciation
    and common problems with management accounts, 186
    definition, 61
    entries in accounting records, 62
    in the balance sheet, 117
    not deductible for tax, 279
    useful economic life concept, 137
desktop software
    advantages, 87
    vs cloud software, 85
Direct Debit
    and sales, 19
distributable profits, 122
dividends, 224
    illegal dividends, 225
    paperwork, 225
    tax aspects, 226
documentary evidence
    of purchases, 24

E

employing staff, 249
    and the payroll process, 37
    employment status and IR35, 252
    mutuality of obligation, concept, 252
    tax aspects, 253
    vs subcontractors, 249
expense claim process, 31
expenses
    definition, 127

F

financial performance
　definition, 79
　monitoring, 177
　ratios, 196
financial performance ratios, 197
　efficiency ratios, 199
　profitability ratios, 197
　relationship between
　　profitability and efficiency,
　　202
financial position
　definition, 80
　ratios, 196
financial position ratios, 204
　gearing, 205
　liquidity ratios, 204
　stability ratios, 205
financial processes
　and internal controls, 91
　documenting and
　　communicating, 83
　examples of, 12
fixed asset management processes,
　58
fixed asset register
　and common problems with
　　management accounts, 187
　and the nominal ledger, 77
　use in managing fixed assets, 61
fixed assets
　buying and selling, 60
　definition, 116
　historic cost or fair value, 221

forecasting
　definition, 82

G

goods despatched note, 20
goods received note, 28
gross payment status
　and the construction industry
　　scheme, 44
gross profit
　definition, 170
　margin, 170

I

income
　definition, 126
income tax and NIC
　calculation of taxable profits,
　　280
intangible assets
　capitalisation of, 221
　management of, 58
internal controls, 90
　definition, 90
　design, 93
　limitations, 94

J

job costing system, 66
　and the sales process, 20
journals, 75

K

key performance indicators (KPI's), 189
   and ratio analysis, 194
   selection of, 191
   types of, 192

L

liabilities
   definition, 118
liquidity
   accounting concept, 109
   and working capital, 200
   meaning, 119
   ratios, 196

M

management accounts
   common problems, 184
   definition, 104
   frequency of production and review, 106
   reviewing, 178
management controls, 91
marketing, 255
   budgeting for costs of, 256
materiality, 148

N

net book value
   of fixed assets, 61
net current assets, 119
net profit
   definition, 172
   margin, 173
NIC
   and tax compliance, 55
nominal accounts, 72
nominal ledger, 70
   and internal controls, 92
   maintenance of, 76
notes to the accounts, 145

O

online banking
   and authority limits, 52
operating profit, 133
   definition, 172
   margin, 172
organisational controls, 91
other operating income, 133

P

password controls
   over access to the nominal ledger, 78
PAYE
   and employing staff, 251
   and subcontractors, 250
   and tax compliance, 55
   control account, 41, 55
   payment due date, 55
   reporting periods, 55
paying yourself, 236

employer pension contributions, 239
salary vs dividends, 237
tax cliff edges, 239
payroll process, 35
and paying employees, 40
and tax compliance, 55
personal bank accounts
use for business purposes, 48
personnel controls, 91
physical controls, 91
over fixed assets, 59
over stock, 65
pre year-end planning, 214
pricing, 241
and the marketing mix, 244
primary financial statements, 99
profit & loss account, 126
and dividends, 224
capital vs revenue expenditure, 136
definition, 100
difference between profits and cash flows, 128
earnings before interest, depreciation, taxation and amortisation (EBITDA), 138
example, 129
in capital & reserves, 122
matching concept, 137
reviewing, 177
taxation not shown in sole trader or partnership accounts, 135
profit margins, 169
and pricing, 243
margin vs mark-up, 173
prudence, 148
purchase ledger, 70
purchase ordering, 27
purchases process, 22
and internal controls, 92
and paying suppliers, 29
selecting suppliers, 26

R

raising finance, 266
angel investment, 269
debt vs equity, 267
grant funding, 274
types of debt finance, 269
ratio analysis, 194
real time stock systems, 66
reliability
of financial statements, 148
retained profits, 122
retained reserves, 122

S

sales invoice
contents of, 17
sales ledger, 70
sales process, 13
segregation of duties, 91
selling a business, 285
selling and distribution costs, 132
share capital, 121
Standing Orders
and sales, 19

statutory accounts
    definition, 103
stock
    and common problems with management accounts, 186
stock management processes, 64
    stock counts, 67
    valuation, 67
substance over form, 148
supervisory controls, 91

T

tangible assets
    management of, 58
tax compliance processes, 53
taxation
    impact on decision making, 275
    importance of timely advice, 277
timeliness
    of financial statements, 149
timesheet system
    and the payroll process, 38
turnover, 131

U

understandability
    of financial statements, 147

V

VAT
    and expense claims, 33
    and recording purchases, 25
    and sales invoices, 18
    and stock valuation, 67
    and tax compliance, 54
    control account, 54
    duplication of input VAT claims, 187
    exclusion from expenses, 132
    exclusion from turnover, 131
    failure to register on time, 247
    inclusion in cash flow projections, 157
    on commercial property, 264
    pre registration VAT, 248
    registration, 245
    voluntary registration, 247

W

working capital
    and bank overdrafts, 271
    and invoice finance, 273
    and pre year end planning, 219
    definition, 200
    key performance indicators (KPI's), 191
    management of, 201, 207
    working capital/ cash conversion cycle, 201